The media's watching Vault!
Here's a sampling of our coverage.

"Unflinching, fly-on-the-wall reports... No one gets past company propaganda to the nitty-gritty inside dope better than these guys."
— *Knight-Ridder newspapers*

"Best way to scope out potential employers...Vault.com has sharp insight into corporate culture and hiring practices."
— *Yahoo! Internet Life*

"Vault.com has become a de facto Internet outsourcer of the corporate grapevine."
— *Fortune*

"For those hoping to climb the ladder of success, [Vault.com's] insights are priceless."
— *Money.com*

"Another killer app for the Internet."
— *New York Times*

"If only the company profiles on the top sites would list the 'real' information... Sites such as Vault.com do this, featuring insights and commentary from employees and industry analysts."
— *The Washington Post*

"A rich repository of information about the world of work."
— *Houston Chronicle*

VAULT
> the insider career network™

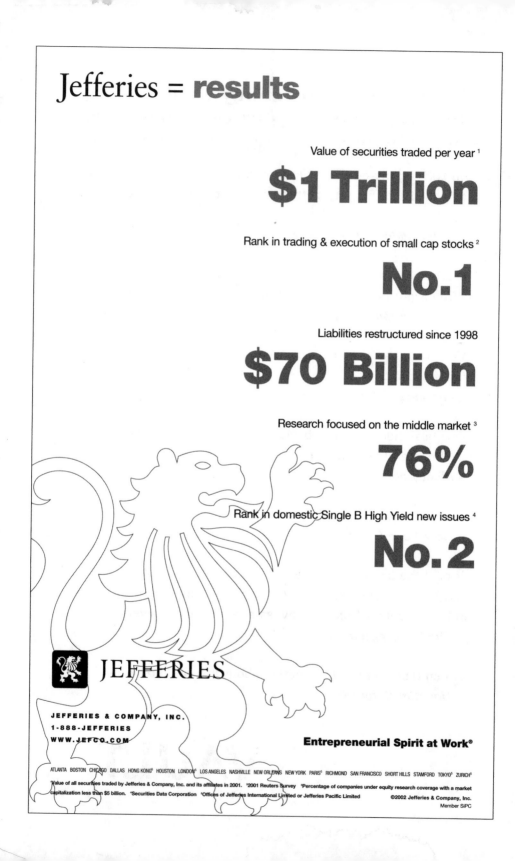

Jefferies = **results**

Value of securities traded per year [1]

$1 Trillion

Rank in trading & execution of small cap stocks [2]

No.1

Liabilities restructured since 1998

$70 Billion

Research focused on the middle market [3]

76%

Rank in domestic Single B High Yield new issues [4]

No.2

JEFFERIES

JEFFERIES & COMPANY, INC.
1-888-JEFFERIES
WWW.JEFCO.COM

Entrepreneurial Spirit at Work®

ATLANTA BOSTON CHICAGO DALLAS HONG KONG[5] HOUSTON LONDON[5] LOS ANGELES NASHVILLE NEW ORLEANS NEW YORK PARIS[5] RICHMOND SAN FRANCISCO SHORT HILLS STAMFORD TOKYO[5] ZURICH[5]

[1]Value of all securities traded by Jefferies & Company, Inc. and its affiliates in 2001. [2]2001 Reuters Survey [3]Percentage of companies under equity research coverage with a market capitalization less than $5 billion. [4]Securities Data Corporation [5]Offices of Jefferies International Limited or Jefferies Pacific Limited

VAULT FINANCE INTERVIEWS PRACTICE GUIDE

Get on the
front line faster.

TD Securities offers excellent opportunities for growth and career development.

Are you a self-starter willing to take on challenges right from the outset? Are you a strong team player interested in becoming a member of a dynamic organization? If so, consider a career at TD Securities - a leading investment dealer with offices in over 20 cities around the globe.

To find out more about us, visit Careers at www.tdsecurities.com.

 Securities

Where Deals Get Done.

> the insider career network™

VAULT FINANCE INTERVIEWS PRACTICE GUIDE

DAVID MONTOYA
AND THE STAFF OF VAULT

All information in this book is subject to change without notice. Vault makes no claims as to
the accuracy and reliability of the information contained within and disclaims all warranties.
No part of this book may be reproduced or transmitted in any form or by any means,
electronic or mechanical, for any purpose, without the express written permission of Vault Inc.

Vault, the Vault logo, and "the insider career network™" are trademarks of Vault Inc.

For information about permission to reproduce selections from this book, contact Vault Inc.,
150 W. 22nd St., 5th Floor, New York, NY 10011, (212) 366-4212.

Library of Congress CIP Data is available.

ISBN 1-58131-170-2

Printed in the United States of America

ACKNOWLEDGEMENTS

Vault would like to acknowledge the assistance and support of Matt Doull, Ahmad Al-Khaled, Lee Black, Eric Ober, Hollinger Ventures, Tekbanc, New York City Investment Fund, American Lawyer Media, Globix, Hoover's, Glenn Fischer, Mark Hernandez, Ravi Mhatre, Carter Weiss, Ken Cron, Ed Somekh, Isidore Mayrock, Zahi Khouri, Sana Sabbagh and other Vault investors. Many thanks to our loving families and friends.

Special thanks to Deborah Adeyanju and Evan Cohen. Thanks also to H.S. Hamadeh, Val Hadjiyski, Marcy Lerner, Chris Prior, Rob Schipano, Jake Wallace, Ed Shen, and Tyya N. Turner and the rest of the Vault staff for their support.

This is Citigroup.

Last year, Jeff learned about derivatives.

This year, he traded $200 Million worth of them.

During a course in investments, something "clicked"–Jeff knew he wanted to become a derivatives trader. A year later, he was helping to conduct some of the biggest trades in the world. Jeff believes this could have only happened at Citigroup. With a revolutionary business model that is quickly changing the industry, Citigroup recruits ambitious, highly talented people and allows them to find their own path to their potential. To find out more, come to one of our on-campus presentations or have a look online. Who knows? It could be one of the best investments you'll ever make. **Citigroup.com**

who benefits most

from your hard work?

That's the question that makes many people consider working for themselves. The freedoms of self-employment offer great choices that affect the quality of your life and the lives of others. You choose with whom you want to work and the level of success to which you aspire. With hard work, your income can be a reflection of your energy, commitment and drive—not someone else's expectations.

With 145 years of industry experience, Northwestern Mutual understands the importance of its Financial Representatives making the right self-employment choices—because success begins with choosing the path that's right for you.

Take the online Self-Employment Screen and explore the opportunities that are most suitable to your personality. Log on to http://careers.nmfn.com and explore "Begin Now."

Send resume to:
resume@northwesternmutual.com

Are you there yet?®

www.nmfn.com

Deloitte & Touche

be there

Deloitte
Touche
Tohmatsu

www.deloitte.com

INTRODUCTION

Do you have an interview coming up with a financial institution?

Unsure how to handle a finance Interview?

Vault Live Finance Interview Prep

Vault brings you a new service to help you prepare for your finance interviews. Your 1-hour live session with a Vault finance expert will include an actual 30-minute finance interview, which will be immediately followed by a 30-minute critique and Q&A session with your expert.

Investment Banking/Corporate Finance Interview Prep

This session preps you for questions about:

- Mergers & acquisitions
- Valuation models
- Accounting concepts
- Personality fit for investment banking and corporate finance positions
- And more!

Sales & Trading Interview Prep

This session prepares you for questions about:

- Capital markets
- Macroeconomics, including impact of different pieces of economic data on securities prices
- Trading strategies
- Interest rates
- Securities including equities, fixed income, currencies, options, and other derivatives
- Personality fit for sales & trading positions
- And more!

For more information go to http://finance.vault.com

> the insider career network™

Practice Makes Perfect

This book is designed to supplement the *Vault Guide to Finance Interviews*. We recommend that you purchase and read that book before reading this one, especially if you have little or no familiarity with finance or the financial services industry.

We have compiled a list of actual questions asked during finance interviews, along with some suggested answers. It's important to stress that these are suggested answers — we don't recommend that you memorize and recite the responses we have provided verbatim. Rather, you should use these for reference.

A guide to this guide

Finance interviews are sometimes conducted by members of the HR team, sometimes by "line professionals" (i.e. actual bankers, traders, or finance department members), and occasionally by various combinations of HR and line professionals in team interview situations.

While there is certainly overlap among the type of questions asked in a particular type of interview, we have organized this guide and the questions into four broad categories.

- **Fit questions and general finance questions.** These questions, found in this Introduction chapter, are commonly asked of all finance interview candidates. They are intended to test a jobseeker's basic level of "fitness" for a finance position in terms of temperament, interest in financial markets, and basic finance knowledge.

- **Corporate finance/M&A questions.** These questions are those commonly faced in investment banking interviews, as well as those found in interviews for an internal corporate finance position. This section will be helpful for those pursuing a career in commercial banking as well.

- **Sales & trading questions.** These questions are applicable to both the sell-side and the buy-side.

- **Research/investment management questions.** These questions are those that one might field both on the buy- and sell-side for a research position.

You may want to browse through more than one of these sections. If you are pursuing a position at a hedge fund, for example, you may find that your position will entail some trading AND research. A general management program at an asset management firm or a rating agency might require some knowledge of all of the above subjects, and so forth. Also, we stress that these categories are basic groupings that reflect the likelihood of a question being asked in a specific type of interview — you may encounter any of these questions in any finance interview, depending on what financial product you're likely to be working with (fixed income vs. equity vs. derivatives, etc.) and how frisky your interviewer is feeling.

The vast majority of the questions in this guide are finance-related (technical) questions that you'd receive in an interview with a line professional. However, we stress that preparing for "fit" questions is vital — in some interviews, even with finance professionals, you may face a greater proportion of these so-called "behavioral" questions. Samples of these questions begin on the next page.

"Fit" Questions

Below are some of the most commonly asked "fit" questions, all of which you should think about before you go into your interviews.

1. Why did you choose to go to _____ college or university?

2. Why did you major in _____?

3. What was your overall GPA (if not on resume)? What was your SAT/GMAT?

4. What courses did you do the best/worst in?

5. Tell me about your college/grad school experience.

6. What appeals to you about this position?

7. Why would you be a good choice for this position? Why should we hire you?

8. What do you think this position requires, and how well do you match those requirements?

9. Why did you leave your last position?

10. What did you learn about yourself at your last job?

11. Describe the most relevant and specific items in your background that show that you are qualified for this job.

12. What matters most to you in your next position?

13. Give me an example where you came with a creative solution to a problem.

14. Give me an example where you successfully persuaded others to think or do what you wanted.

15. Give me an example where you sought out a problem to solve because it represented a challenge for you.

16. Give me examples of your leadership abilities.

17. Describe a project in which you went beyond what was expected of you.

18. What events have had the most significant impact on your life?

19. What motivates you?

20. What kind of activities do you enjoy?

21. Discuss something about yourself that I cannot learn from your resume.

22. Tell me about your reasons for selecting this industry.

23. What is it about our company that interests you?

24. Describe what would be an ideal environment for you?

25. What would you do if you did not have to work for money? How does that relate to this job opportunity?

26. How do you define stress and how do you manage it?

27. Describe your ideal job.

28. Give examples of how you have used your greatest skills.

29. What is your major weakness?

30. What have been your major successes and accomplishments? How did you achieve these?

31. What were your failures and what did you learn from them?

32. What role do you usually take in a team?

33. Do you have any questions for me?

34. Tell me your biggest regret.

Because the answers to these types of questions will vary depending on the person, we've focused on answers to technical questions in this guide. However, you will find some sample answers to behavioral questions later in this guide. We do suggest that you write out answers to at least some of the above questions as well as to the questions contained later on in this book.

Write up some answers to these common fit questions. Looking over your own answers to typical questions will prove helpful before an interview. We have all walked out of interviews thinking "God! Why didn't I say _____ when s/he asked ____!" Thinking about potential questions before interviews will make you seem less nervous and more polished, and help you land the finance job of your dreams.

Sample "Fit" Questions and Answers

1. Why do you want to work here?

This question is designed to demonstrate how much research you have done on the firm as well as to see if you might be a good "fit." To get further information about a particular firm, you should read recent press stories, visit their web page, and also read the Vault guide written about it. This answer should be based on your actual reasons; you don't want to get caught in a lie. You should still manage to show that you know a bit about the firm, its people, its culture, and its specialties in your answer. For example, you might want to emphasize your desire for strong team mentality at virtually all of the banks (but especially Goldman). If you are interviewing at a firm where entry-level financial analyst and associate-level hires go through a rotation program before getting placed, you might want to emphasize that you like the fact that one can see more than one area before a final decision is made. (Note: for summer internships, some firms will rotate you through two areas of the banking department.)

Other things to know and weave into your answer include: Is the firm a small firm and ostensibly hoping to stay small or trying to get bigger? Is the structure flat with few layers of management or are there several titles between analyst and managing director? Is the firm part of a commercial bank or is it a pure brokerage and investment bank? If you are interviewing for an internal corporate finance position, do you have to (or can you) rotate through various finance and/or non-financial parts of the business (marketing, sales, etc.)?

Most important, you should emphasize the people. Many banking professionals maintain that things are the same no matter where you work, but the people you work with can have very different personalities. You should have met at least three people whose names and titles you can recite at the interview; five to ten would be even better, even if they were not all in the corporate finance or M&A departments. You should discuss why you like the people you've met and why this makes you want to become part of the team.

It is good to talk about the firm's culture, but not okay to blatantly state that you want to work for a prestigious firm (for reasons similar to why you should not discuss wanting to make money).

2. What skills can you bring to the table?

Your answer should match the desired skills mentioned above. If you have no financial or analytical background, discuss any accounting, finance or economics courses you have taken, or ways in which you have analyzed problems at school or in past jobs. Talk about any personal investing you have done through E*Trade or Schwab. Emphasize any activities involving a great deal of dedication and endurance you have participated in. (Have you run a marathon, did you participate in a sport, were you in the Peace Corps or the military, did you train for years to be a top ballerina?)

3. What about you might be a disadvantage at this firm?

This is a variation of the old "weakness" question. You should find a weakness that you can turn into a positive. For example, driving yourself too hard or putting the needs of others before your own too often.

4. At what other firms are you looking?

This is another key question. Even if you are looking at every major Wall Street firm, and a few minor ones, your interviewer wants to hear that you are focused, and they hear this by you (truthfully) stating that you are talking to similar firms. For example, Morgan Stanley probably wants to hear that you are talking to Goldman or Merrill (bulge-bracket). Merrill probably wants to hear Morgan Stanley, Goldman, or Citigroup SSB. Bear would want to hear Lehman, CSFB, or Citigroup/SSB (similar cultures at CSFB and SSB, similar smaller-firm feel at Lehman). Bank of America sees itself as the next Citigroup, and so forth. There is no correct answer, since every interviewer is different. However, if you tell Goldman that you are interviewing only at Goldman and Bear Stearns but are not interested in Morgan Stanley, or you tell Citigroup/SSB that it is between them and Lazard, your interviewer may look at you askance.

That said, the more "wanted" you are by other firms, the more desirable you will appear to your interviewer. If you are interviewing at 12 firms, all else being equal your interviewer will take more notice than if you are interviewing at just two. If a prestigious firm seems interested in you, by all means let this be known. This also improves your cachet. Do not lie about any of this, however, since recruiters do talk to each other and you may end up blackballed across the Street.

If you are interviewing at both the banks and for internal finance jobs, you may want to mention this to the banks. Your first choice is always to be wherever you are interviewing. Always.

5. How would you say our firm compares to these others: _____?

This is designed to show your overall knowledge of the industry. You should demonstrate how much you know about the firm you are interviewing with and its competition without insulting or being overly critical of another firm. Bad-mouthing another bank is considered poor form.

6. What are the major criteria that you will use to select an employer?

This should match your response to the "Why have chosen this firm?" question.

7. Where do you expect to be in 5 years? In 10 years?

This question can be asked in any interview, but the interviewer is looking for you to show that you have a genuine interest in the markets and research. Thus, stating that you want to be a top analyst or strategist or a managing director in five years shows ambition, and saying that you may want to start your own hedge fund in 10 to 15 years is not out of line. Saying that you hope to make a quick million and then become a filmmaker does not sound so good.

Basic Finance Questions

1. What do you think is going to happen with interest rates over the next six months?

This is another way of asking "What has the market been doing? What do you think the market will do in the coming 12 months?"

If you have been reading *The Wall Street Journal*, *The Economist*, analyst reports etc., this should not pose a problem. If not, start reading them today.

2. What is a bulge bracket firm?

"Bulge bracket" is a term that loosely translates into the largest full service brokerages/investment banks as measured by various league table standings. Goldman Sachs, Morgan Stanley and Merrill Lynch are considered the ultimate examples (sometimes called the "Super Bulge Bracket") Of late, Citigroup/Salomon Smith Barney, CSFB and, increasingly, J.P. Morgan Chase are considered to have joined the U.S. bulge bracket. Globally, J.P. Morgan Chase, Deutsche Bank and UBS Warburg/PaineWebber are typically thrown in with the U.S. top five to form the so-called "Global Bulge Bracket." (Outside of the U.S., Deutsche Bank, J.P. Morgan and UBS frequently outrank Goldman in the league tables, for example.)

If you are at a bulge bracket firm, you believe that only the very largest and niche firms will survive over the next few years. If you are applying to a bulge bracket aspirant (DB and UBS for a U.S.-based position; Bank of America, Lehman, Bear, ABN Amro, DKW, or BNP Paribas globally) you want to demonstrate your knowledge of how the firm at which you are interviewing is moving up various league tables and will soon join the ranks of the "Global Bulge Brackets." Or how the firm is essentially already a bulge bracket firm in many areas. Or how you want to be part of a firm with room for growth. If you are interviewing with a boutique or regional firm (Lazard, TWP or Jefferies, at the time of publication), you should emphasize your belief that firms able to carve out a niche and build strong relationships will survive and even thrive.

3. How do you stay on top of the markets?

You want to demonstrate that you read the key publications (and, you should). *The Wall Street Journal*, the *Financial Times*, *The Economist*, and *BusinessWeek* should be on your reading list. You should watch CNBC, Bloomberg Television, and CnnFn. You will get bonus points for reading analysts' research reports (especially of the firm at which you are interviewing).

4. Where and what is the Dow? Where are the 1-year, 5-year, and 10-year Treasury? What is the price of gold? Where is the S&P 500? Where is the US trade deficit?

They really do ask these sorts of questions, especially of people from non-financial backgrounds. You should keep track of these and other key financial numbers on at least a weekly basis. While you do not have to be exact, if you say that the NASDAQ is around 12,000 and the Nikkei is about 400, your attempt to convince Merrill that you are really interested in global finance will fall short.

5. What is unique about the U.S. treasury market vs. the rest of the debt market?

The U.S. Federal government's bonds are considered riskless, since the U.S. has never defaulted and is the world's strongest economy. All other bonds trade at and are quoted at a certain percentage or "basis" over treasuries (except in the case of a few other AAA-rated countries like France or the U.K.).

6. What is "junk?"

Called "high-yield" bonds by the investment banks (never call it junk yourself), these bonds are below investment grade, and are generally unsecured debt. Below investment grade means at or below BB (by Standard & Poor's) or Ba (by Moody's). Some less credit worthy companies issue debt at high yields because they have difficulty in securing bank debt or in tapping the equity markets.

Sometimes high yield debt starts out investment grade and then "crosses over" to high yield. (Think of K-Mart or the Gap, which had their ratings lowered in 2002.) Bonds from extremely high credit risk companies, like Enron in early 2002, are categorized as "distressed debt."

7. Tell me what the repeal of Glass-Steagall means to me as a capital markets participant.

This sort of question is aimed at finding out how much in-depth market knowledge you have. If you claim that you have always followed or have always been interested in the markets, but can't answer a question along these lines, you may be in trouble.

What is commonly referred to as the Glass-Steagall law is actually the Bank Act of 1933, which erected a wall between commercial banking and securities/brokerage. Commercial banking and insurance were separated by the Bank Holding Company act of 1956. The Gramm-Leach-Bliley Act repealed these laws in 1999.

What the repeal has done is pave the way in the U.S. for so-called "Universal Banks" and what Europeans sometimes call "Bankassurance" firms. While the Europeans always allowed such firms to exist, the U.S. (until 1999) and the Japanese have forbidden them. Examples of truly universal banks (investment banks as well as insurance companies and full-fledged commercial banks) include Citigroup/SSB, Credit Suisse/CSFB, Allianz/Dresdner Kleinwort Wasserstein, and ABN AMRO. Firms that have both investment and commercial banks include J.P. Morgan Chase, Bank of America, Deutsche Bank, and UBS. Goldman, Merrill, Morgan Stanley, Lehman, and Bear are "still" pure brokerage firms, for the most part.

Many believe the recent consolidation wave (Travelers/Citibank, Dresdner/Wasserstein/Allianz, Credit Suisse/DLJ, UBS/PaineWebber, J.P. Morgan/Chase) will result in the inevitable merger of these last few "holdouts" merging with a large commercial bank and/or an insurance company. Many believe that having a large balance sheet and numerous corporate banking relationships will increasingly allow universal banks to use loans and their other relationships to gain greater market share in higher-margin areas like M&A and underwriting. Indeed, Citibank and to a lesser extent J.P. Morgan and Bank of America have moved up in several league tables. ABN AMRO and

Allianz/Dresdner have slipped by some measures, and the jury is still out on how much being a full-service firm has helped some others. The results are similarly mixed for the pure brokers, though many point to the huge losses made by Citigroup and J.P. Morgan Chase on loans to Enron and Global Crossing as proof that a balance sheet does not always help. Some have speculated that J.P. Morgan may lose more on bad loans to Enron than it has made in investment banking fees for that client and several others combined. In any event, J.P. Morgan's CEO recently acknowledged that such a strategy is risky.

The bottom line is: If you are talking to a pure brokerage firm like Goldman, you want to spell out the threat from universal banks, but stress that pure brokerage can and will succeed. If you are at Bank of America, you believe universal banks are the wave of the future.

8. Tell me three major investment banking industry trends and describe them briefly.

Here are four possible answers:

I. Consolidation: More firms are teaming up. Examples include: Citibank and Travelers/SSB, Morgan Stanley/Dean Witter, Deutsche Banc/Alex. Brown, BNP/Paribas, Dresdner/Wasserstein/Allianz, Credit Suisse/DLJ, UBS/PaineWebber, Merrill Lynch and brokerages in the U.K., Canada, Australia, Japan, Spain, and South Africa, J.P. Morgan and Chase... all driven largely by the need to increase capital base and geographic reach.

II. Expansion in Europe: More U.S. firms see the ending of corporate cross-holdings, increasing use of capital markets to raise financing along with pension reform as leading to greater growth opportunities for their European-based businesses.

III. Technology: Increasingly, firms are using ECN (Electronic Communication Networks, like Archipelago, Island or Instinet) to route and execute trades. Even in traditional forms of trading, technology is lowering costs but simultaneously lowering margins and commoditising many markets. In addition, increasingly sophisticated derivative and risk management products and distribution of information have been made possible due to recent advances in computing and telecommunications technology.

IV. Demographic shift: The "baby boomers" in all of the advanced industrial countries are nearing retirement. Simultaneously, the boomers' parents and grandparents will leave their estates to their children and grandchildren, leading to the single greatest inter-generational transfer of wealth the world has ever seen. Over the next few decades there should therefore be a sharp rise in the demand for investment services products to support these "Boomers" through retirement years around the world.

9. What is a hedge fund?

Hedge funds are loosely regulated investment pools (they are limited partnerships). They generally are open only to the wealthy or institutions. Hedge funds use many strategies to hedge against risk with the goal of making a profit in any market environment. Hedge funds may short stock, use leverage, options, futures, or employ a risk arbitrage strategy, among other things. Hedge funds, though, do not always hedge or sell short. Some funds had virtually all of their money long during the bull market of the late 1990s, for example. What unifies hedge funds is the fact that, unlike mutual funds, they can invest in whatever they please (as long as it is legal) and do not have to issue prospectuses or follow other limits and regulations that mutual fund mangers must. In addition, they usually charge much higher fees than traditional fund managers. Finally, they are limited to less than 500 or 100 investors (depending on how they are structured), whereas a mutual fund can have thousands of investors. While hedge funds usually have less under management than a traditional institutional investor, the fact that they trade relatively often makes them valuable customers for brokerage firms.

10. Why do we care about housing starts?

The housing industry accounts for over 25% of investment spending in the U.S. and approximately 5% of U.S. GDP. The housing starts figure is considered a leading indicator. Housing starts rise before an economic uptick, and decline before a slow down.

11. What has the market been doing? Why? What do you think the market will do in coming 12 months?

If you have been reading your business publications, you should be able to answer this question in an informed manner.

12. What is the difference between senior and junior bondholders?

Senior bondholders get paid first (and as a result their bonds pay a lower rate of interest if all else is equal). The order in which debtors get paid in the case of bankruptcy is generally: commercial debts (vendors), mortgage lenders, other bank lenders, senior secured bondholders, subordinated (junior) secured bondholders, debentures (unsecured) holders, preferred stock holders, and finally straight equity (stockholders.)

13. What is the best story you read this week in *The Wall Street Journal*?

This question can ruin an otherwise great interview. The interviewer is trying find out if you read more than just the front page of the *Journal*, and that you read it fairly regularly. It does not have to be a story that shows your depth of knowledge about the market; it could be a human-interest story. If you don't remember a recent *WSJ* story, try recounting a *BusinessWeek*, *The Economist*, or even a CNBC story.

14. Tell me about some stocks you follow. Should I buy any of them?

This question often comes up in sales & trading or research interviews (often posed as, "Sell me a stock") but it can also come up in banking interviews to test your general market knowledge. You may find that as you begin to talk about Viacom or GM the interviewer will interrupt you and ask for a small-cap or non-U.S. name instead. Your best bet is to be prepared with knowledge of at least four varied companies: A large cap U.S. Company, a small-cap U.S. company, a non-U.S. company and a short-sell pitch (or a stock you would recommend an investor sell rather than buy).

You should try to read a few analysts reports and press stories on your companies. At the very least you should know the name, ticker symbol, the CEO's name, a brief description of the company's line of business, and three points supporting your argument (if you feel strongly that one should buy or sell). You should also know who (if anyone) covers the stock at the firm you are interviewing with and their rating. You should be able to recite (if asked) the basic valuation metrics (P/E, growth rate, etc.). You should also be prepared to answer common criticisms of your pitch (if you believe that one should buy or sell the stock). ("Isn't GM in an industry facing overcapacity?" "Yes, but according to your firm's auto analyst, management has succeeded in streamlining costs and increasing profitability...", etc.)

The point is not to be correct or agree with the interviewer or their firm's analyst, but to be persuasive and demonstrate your knowledge of the markets.

Be prepared. Be very, very prepared.

Make sure you're prepared for your finance interviews with Vault's Career Guides and Career Services at the Vault Finance Career Channel. Go to http://finance.vault.com.

- For sample questions and overviews of important finance concepts, get the *Vault Guide to the Finance Interview* and the *Vault Guide to Advanced and Quantitative Finance Interviews*.

- For insider information about top employers, get the *Vault Guide to the Top 50 Finance Employers*, and Vault's Finance Employer Profiles, our 50-page reports on top firms, including Goldman Sachs, Morgan Stanley, Merrill, CSFB, J.P. Morgan Chase, Salomon Smith Barney, UBS Warburg and many more.

- For expert advice on specific careers, get the *Vault Career Guide to Investment Banking*, the *Vault Career Guide to Investment Management*, the *Vault Career Guide to Venture Capital*, and other Vault industry career guides.

- For one-on-one coaching with a finance interview expert, get Vault's Finance Interview Prep.

CORPORATE FINANCE AND M&A

Skills for Corporate Finance/M&A

This section is designed to help prepare you for both internal finance positions (for example, at Disney or IBM) and for external positions with investment banks. One thing any applicant for a corporate finance or mergers and acquisitions ("M&A") position should understand is that there are particular skills the interviewer is trying to ferret out.

These include so-called "people skills." Most professionals below the Managing Director/EVP/Partner level are expected to put in long and intense hours (especially at investment banks). Your interviewer is going to ask him or herself, "Is this someone I can work late nights and travel with every day for the next few years without us getting on each others nerves? Is this someone who can pull two consecutive all-nighters, shower, and give a proposal to a Fortune 500 CFO the next day?" As such, those who can be in turns outgoing and friendly and reserved and professional tend to do better than those who come across as shy or abrasive. In addition, there are other skills sought by interviewers for these sorts of positions. In other words, your interviewer will seek to discover:

- Can you analyze appropriate financing, acquisition and investment possibilities for a (your) company?

- Will you be able to evaluate and scrutinize existing and potential corporate clients and industries in order to match the appropriate security with a financing need?

- Can you go long periods with little activity and then quickly ramp up to work effectively under extreme pressure while managing multiple deadlines?

- Will you come up with new project ideas while being imaginative and resourceful?

- Does your interviewer see you joining and contributing to concurrent teams of both a project and cross-functional nature?

- Do you mind frequent travel? Even if it means five cities in two days?

- Can you assess potential outcomes related to strategic and pecuniary choices made by a (your) firm?

- Do you have prior financial, banking, accounting or mergers and acquisitions experience?

- Do you have the wherewithal to work at 100% for 80-100+ hours a week for weeks on end? Even at the expense of your personal life?

- Are you capable of assessing business line and divisional results versus a (your) company's target?

- Can you evaluate a (your) firm's relative position?

- Will you be able to analyze and quickly understand single company information, industry-wide issues, and how they might be affected by macro-economic trends?

- Are you good at building ongoing relationships with, and getting information from, company management, research analysts, capital markets professionals, lawyers, (other firms') bankers and others with whom you will have regular contact?

- Can you alternate between being courteous, professional, gregarious, and sycophantic with all types of people, from secretaries to CEOs?

- Are you very good at financial modeling and valuation, especially when using Excel?

- Do you understand various valuation methods and procedures (discounted cash flow techniques, WACC, free cash flow, comparable analysis, and sensitivity analysis, etc.)?

- Are you an expert at accounting? Can you quickly analyze financial statements quantitatively and qualitatively?

- Will you be able to accurately project earnings, cash flow statements and balance sheets trends?

- Do you have exceptional presentation, selling and marketing skills in both formal and informal setting?

- Will you eventually be able to bring in new business to the firm?

- Are you a stickler for detail and extremely well organized?

- Are you personally passionate about the market?

Below are some specific questions asked during past Corporate Finance/M&A interviews along with possible answers.

Corporate Finance/M&A Questions

1. Why Corporate Finance or M&A (or both if applicable)?

There are several good responses to this question, and you should tailor your response so that it is truthful and fits in with your goals. If you are interviewing for pure M&A or corporate finance positions at banks as well as rotational programs or internal corporate finance positions, you should be honest about this, although your first choice is always to be wherever you are interviewing.

While you should not lie, you should omit any consulting, marketing or other completely unrelated interviews you may have lined up. Employers (especially the banks) want dedication. You should also make certain that your answers mesh with the desired skills mentioned earlier in this chapter. You should also not state that you want internal corporate finance because you think the hours are better than in investment banking (even though they are generally) because you don't want to come across as lazy.

If you are going for a particular group or function, you should not deride an area you are not interested in. Many who aspired to be technology M&A bankers and started in 2001 or 2002 found themselves working on food industry corporate finance deals (if they were lucky enough to keep their jobs). Most banks place new associates in particular areas only if they have expertise (i.e. someone who worked at Disney before business school in the media group or a medical doctor in healthcare). Financial analysts are even less likely to get the group they want. Most likely, you will end up wherever there is an opening.

One questionable response is that you want to make a lot of money. There are successful banking professionals who have said this in interviews and lived to tell about it, but most would advise against it unless the interviewer brings it up first. Even then it should be only one of many reasons why you want to work for a firm. The reason often given for this taboo is the idea that firms are looking for future leaders and team members, not those out for a quick buck. Of course, everyone knows Wall Street pays astronomical sums even to those just out of business school or a few years out of undergrad, and a good portion of the people interviewing you would not be working on the Street were it not for their 6-8 figure paychecks. It is, however, an unwritten rule that money is not discussed in an interview. This seems to be truer at "white shoe" firms like Goldman, Morgan Stanley and J.P. Morgan than at Bear or Citigroup/SSB.

2. What is different about an internal finance position versus working as an investment banker?

The basic skills necessary for a successful career in internal finance are generally the same as those required to be a thriving banker. Depending on the company and the exact job function, your day-to-day activities in an internal finance position might vary widely. Here are just some possible differences.

Specific industry knowledge: As a banker, you might start as a generalist or be part of a functional team (mergers and acquisitions, structured finance, relationship management), a geographic team (emerging markets, Latin America, Germany) and/or an industry group (media and telecommunications, health care, financial institutions). Even so, your work will be largely transaction-based; that is, you will "do a deal" for one client, then one for another, and then another, and so on. Even if you specialize by industry, the individual company dynamics will vary from deal to deal.

In contrast, an internal finance professional will gain a much greater understanding of his or her company or individual business line, since he or she will likely work exclusively in one area for a longer period of time. For example, a media and telecommunications banker will get a better a bird's eye view of AOL Time Warner's finances while working on a bond offering than one of AOL's home video division financial analysts. Conversely, the banker will probably never learn as much about DVD sales. Similarly, someone working in AOL's treasury department will gain an even greater understanding of the company's finances than either the home video financial analyst or the banker. However, the treasury department employee will likely also know less about DVD sales than the analyst, and less about issues facing other media and telecommunications companies than the banker.

Variety of job functions: Again, as a banker, you might be a generalist, or work in a functional, geographic, and/or industry group. These groups all tend to be transaction-oriented.

In an internal finance role, there are several completely different roles in most large companies. In a strategic planning and analysis position at a computer firm like IBM, you might look at the performance of different groups, divisions, and business lines, and decide which ones have performed up to expectations. Based on this and other factors, you might then help decide how to allocate the company's capital going forward. (For example: Maybe the company should try to increase sales in one country, exit one product line altogether, and buy a company in an entirely new business.) You might then set a plan against which one could later judge the company's performance. Another IBM finance employee might spend her time examining the financial statements of companies that IBM wants to sell products to, in order to determine credit risk and credit exposure and ultimately whether or not IBM should provide financing for the sale. A third financial staff member might spend part of his time acting as a sort of internal corporate and investment banker, structuring major financing deals for IBM customers, and then syndicating these deals in much the same way Citigroup or Bank of America would a loan. A fourth might work in IBM's treasury department and assist in managing the company's cash and investments, like an internal investment manager.

Some internal finance professionals will spend all of their time at a company in one area or function, but many large companies will (formally or informally) rotate finance professionals through several such areas over the course of their career. Of course, there are positions in loan syndication, planning and analysis, and credit risk management at the investment banks, but one generally must interview for each of these positions separately from each other and from investment banking.

Risk, rewards and lifestyle: It is no big secret that investment bankers put in long hours and frequently must put their personal lives on hold ("The client doesn't care that you have a wedding to go to. This merger needs to go through while the stock is still near it's all-time high.") It should also come as no surprise that those who go into banking tend to get higher salaries than their peers in internal finance (especially in junior and mid-level positions).

Unless you are working for a start-up, those who work in general finance have somewhat greater job security and do not usually have to work 80 to 100 hours a week or travel on a regular basis.

Does it equal out? That depends on your priorities. It is not surprising that, given the level of endurance and commitment one needs to be an investment banker, those in internal finance positions are more likely to have come from banking than the other way around (again, particularly at the junior- and mid-level). On the other hand, spending any time as a junior banker might be too high of a price for some.

3. Let's say retail sales figures just came out, and they were far below what economists were expecting. What will this do to stock prices and the strength of the dollar?

Bad news might drive the market lower, but if interest rates have been relatively high, such news may lead the Street to expect the Federal Reserve to ease monetary policy, which actually may be bullish for the stock market. Since bad economic news usually leads to the Fed easing interest rates, the dollar will weaken versus most leading foreign currencies, and U.S. companies may benefit, all else being equal.

4. How do you value a bond?

The value of a bond comes derived from the present value of the expected payments or cash flows from a bond, discounted at an interest rate that reflects the default risk associated with the cash flows.

To find the present value of a bond, the formula is:

$$\text{PV of a Bond} = \sum_{t=1}^{t=N} \frac{\text{Coupon}_t}{(1+r)^t} + \frac{\text{Face Value}}{(1+r)^N}$$

Where: Coupon_t = coupon expected in period t, Face Value = the face value of the bond, N = number of periods (usually years or half-years) and r = the discount rate for the cash flows.

For example, let us say that you had an 8% coupon, 30-year maturity bond with a par (face) value of $1,000 that pays its coupons twice a year. If the interest rate on the bond has changed from the coupon (to 10%), one would value the bond thusly:

$$\text{PV of a Bond} = \sum_{1}^{t=60} \frac{40}{(1.05)^t} + \frac{1000}{(1.05)^{60}}$$

The equation can be written out as $40 x Annuity Factor (5%, 60) + $1,000 x PV Factor (5%, 60) = $757.17 + 53.54 = $810.71. These calculations can be done on any standard financial calculator. (Enter n = 60, PMT = 40, FV = 1,000, interest rate = 10%, and then hit the PV button. You should get –810.71 for present value, which is negative because one has to pay this amount to own the bond.)

The discount rate depends upon default risk. Higher rates are used for more risky bonds and lower rates for safer ones. Rating agencies like Standard & Poor's or Moody's assign a rating to bonds. High rated bonds like U.S. Treasuries generally pay the lowest rates, while higher risk bonds (like, say those of an Argentinean steel company) pay higher rates.

If the bond is traded and thus has a market price, one can compute the internal rate of return (IRR) for the bond (the rate at which the present value of the coupons and the face value is equal to the market price.) This is commonly called the yield to maturity on the bond. Unfortunately, IRR and YTM must be computed by trial and error, although financial calculators have functions for computing this.

While you will most likely never have to calculate the value of a bond in a sales and trading interview by hand, it is important to intuitively understand how a bond is valued. Another way to think of it is as follows: suppose you have two credit cards through your local bank, a Visa, which charges you 10% a year, and a MasterCard, which charges 20%. You owe $10,000 on each and can transfer all of your debt to one or another. Which would you choose? Clearly you would put your debt on the Visa. Now, which card would your bank rather you use? $20,000 in debt on the MasterCard at 20% is clearly worth more to the bank. Bonds work the same way. They, like credit card receivables for a bank, represent future interest payments for bondholders. Higher rates for the same value increase the expected present value for an issue all else being equal.

5. What is the difference between preferred stock and regular stock?

Unlike regular (common) stock, preferred stock not only provides the security's owner with an equity stake in the company, but also provides certain bond-like qualities for the owner. Preferred shares usually pay a dividend. Unlike bond yields, preferred yields can be changed or cut, though they are generally cut after common dividends are halted. Should a company run into financial trouble or go bankrupt, preferred holders have a right to earnings and assets after bondholders but before common stockholders. As with its bonds, riskier companies must pay a relatively higher yield on its preferred stock in order to attract investors.

Preferred stock frequently has a conversion option imbedded allowing one to trade in the security for common stock. (See the question on pricing convertible bonds, no. 14 in this chapter.) Institutions are the main purchasers of preferred stock. Companies issue preferred stock for a number of reasons, including the fact that companies view it as a "cheaper" form of financing than common equity, and that it can be constructed so that it is viewed as equity by the rating agencies and debt by the tax authorities.

(Note: Do *not* confuse this with "Class A" versus "Class B" stock or the like. Lettered classes of stock refer to voting and non-voting shares.)

6. What is disintermediation?

According to the original usage of the term as listed in the Oxford Dictionary, it means "a reduction in the use or role of banks and savings institutions as intermediaries between lenders and borrowers; the transfer of savings and borrowings away from the established banking system."

Of late, the term has taken on new meanings as it relates to the world of finance. The word means literally to remove intermediaries from the trading process, so that buyers can deal more directly with sellers. This is also known as "cutting out the middleman." Disintermediation is a hot buzzword in many areas ("eBay is a tool for disintermediation"; direct selling also affects insurance companies and travel agencies). The term was particularly in vogue when B2B was all the rage.

In the banking and brokerage business, many firms have seen traditional customers move towards trading directly with the public by telephone or the Internet (such as when using Ameritrade, or when buying a mutual fund directly from Fidelity or a C.D. from a new online bank rather than at your local branch). Disintermediation is occurring even with corporate and institutional clients: U.S. Treasury securities are often traded electronically without the use of a human trader or brokerage firm, and certain large corporations have issued securities directly to investors without the use of an investment bank. All of this is lowering costs but simultaneously lowering margins and commoditising many markets for investment banks (and their clients).

7. How would you value a stock or a company?

Three common methods used are: Discounted cash flow valuation (DCF), which values a company based on the present value of expected future cash flows produced by that asset (like valuing a bond in a previous question); Relative valuation, which estimates value by looking at the price of "comparable" companies' equity via common ratios such as price/earnings, enterprise value/EBITDA, or price/book value; and "Real Option" theory, which utilizes option pricing models.

To estimate the value using DCF, one can either measure cash flows in the form of free cash flows to the firm (or FCFF, which includes the value of cash flows eventually payable to debt and equity holders and thus values the whole company), dividends (the "dividend discount valuation" or DDV), or free cash flows to equity (FCFE; DDV and FCFE value only the company's equity). Regardless of which method one chooses, the DCF method is essentially the same as valuing a bond:

$$\text{Value} = \sum_{t=1}^{t=n} \frac{CF_t}{(1+r)^t} + \frac{\text{Face Value}}{(1+r)^N}$$

Where CF_t = the cash flow in period t, r = discount rate (determined by the risk level of the cash flows in question) and t = the life of the asset.

When valuing a company using the dividend discount method (which is generally now only considered appropriate in valuing financial services companies), the "CF" would be dividends, while the discount rate would be the cost of equity for the asset. When valuing cash flows to equity, one would also use the cost of equity (or K_e) for the discount rate. When valuing cash flows to the firm, one would use the weighted average cost of capital (or WACC, which is the weighted cost of the firm's equity and debt) for the discount rate.

The various cash flows can be determined as follows:

Dividends = Net Income x Payout Ratio, while the expected growth in dividends = Retention Ratio x Return on Equity.

Free Cash Flow to Equity = Net Income - (Capital Expenditures - Depreciation) x (1- Debt to Capital Ratio) - Change in Working Capital x

(1- Debt to Capital Ratio) while the expected growth in FCFE = Retention Ratio x Return on Equity.

Free Cash Flow to Firm = Earnings Before Interest and Taxes x (1-tax rate) - (Capital Expenditures - Depreciation) - Change in Working Capital, while expected growth in FCFF = Reinvestment Rate x Return on Firm Capital.

The appropriate discount rates can be determined as follows:

Cost of Equity = Appropriate Risk Free Rate + Beta x Equity Risk Premium

WACC = [Cost of Equity x (Market Value of Equity/Market Value of Equity and Debt)] + [Cost of Debt x (1-Tax Rate) x (Market Value of Debt/Market Value of Equity and Debt)]

The risk free rate must match the firm's cash flows. In the U.S., the risk free rate would be the U.S. Treasury rate with the most similar maturity, while in the Euro-zone it would be a German (or maybe French) government bond, and so forth. Beta is a measure of how changes in a firm's stock price deviate from changes in the market. (In the U.S., usually either the S&P 500 or the Wilshire Total Market Index is used as a measure of the "market.")

Beta is thus the responsiveness of a security to macroeconomic events. High betas can be found in technology companies, smaller firms or in highly cyclical industries, while lower betas would be found in steady industries like grocery chains or tobacco companies (since in good or bad times people eat and smoke.)

For valuation purposes, beta can be historical beta (which can be found using data services like Bloomberg or Yahoo! Finance) or the "Bottom-Up" method which is based on the firm's peers' beta and the firm's leverage (debt level). The "Bottom-Up" method should be used unless the company in question has no real publicly traded peers (like Eurotunnel or the Boston Celtics) or is a financial services firm.

The equity risk premium is either the historical or presently implied level of average return investors demand over the risk-free rate in order to invest in stocks. No two analysts or finance professors use the same number for this, but we will say here that stocks in U.S. generally earn 4.5 percentage points above long-term U.S. Treasuries. The risk premium would be higher for emerging market countries. The cost (and value) of debt can be estimated using either the market interest rate on the firm's outstanding debt or the borrowing rate associated with firms that have the same debt rating as the company in question. If these two methods cannot be used, use the borrowing rate and debt rating associated with firms which have the similar financial ratio values (such as EBITA/Debt Expense, also called the interest coverage ratio) to the company in question. Once the rate is known, all debt on the books can be valued at this rate like a bond. In the above WACC formula, we assume that interest is tax deductible (thus the "1-Tax Rate").

When valuing a firm using any DCF method, one must assume that the firm is either steadily growing and will remain this way forever (like a typical grocery store chain), or that it will for a few years grow at a faster rate than the growth of the overall GDP and then will abruptly begin steady growth (like some automobile companies), or that it will grow fast and then gradually move towards steady growth (like a technology company).

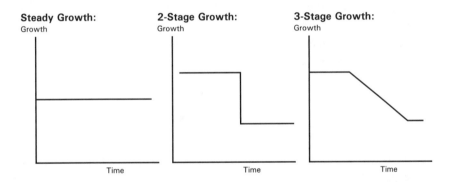

To value a company growing forever at the same rate, one would simply value the estimated future cash flows using the above formula. For 2- stage growth companies, one must estimate the NPV of the cash flows over the high growth stage, and then add the NPV of perpetual steady growth based on cash flows at the end of the high growth period (called the terminal value) to this amount. For 3-stage growth companies one must also compute the NPV for each of the intervening years between high and steady growth and add this to the value.

Now, let us take a simple example of using the FCFF method. We will use a fictitious U.S. publicly traded manufacturing company (Vault Machines, Inc.). where earnings are in steady growth forever (5% a year; we are using nominal values for all measures; if you use "real" measures taking into account inflation, you must do so throughout). The company has bonds with a $1 billion market value and no other debt. These bonds currently trade at 10% (which is also par). The 10-year U.S. Treasury is trading at 5%. The firm, like others in its industry, has a marginal tax rate of 40%. The firm just reported revenues for the most recent year of $1 billion and earnings of $50 million. Depreciation expenses were $25 million, and working capital increased by $10 million. The firm purchased a factory for $30 million and made no other capital expenditures during the year. Companies in Vault Machine's same industry have an average Beta of 1.2 and an average debt/equity ratio of 25%. The firm currently has 100 million shares of stock outstanding trading at $20 a share. Is this the appropriate value of the firm's stock? What about for the entire company?

First we will determine the free cash flow to the firm:

Free Cash Flow to Firm = Earnings Before Interest and Taxes x (1-tax rate) - (Capital Expenditures - Depreciation) - Change in Working Capital

EBIT in this case can be found as follows: Since the tax rate is 40%, and the firm earned $50 million after taxes, earnings before taxes = 50/(1-.4) = $83.33 million. We know the firm has $1 billion (market value) in debt outstanding and is paying 10%, thus interest expense = $100 million. Adding interest expense, we get EBIT = $183.33 million.

FCFF = 183.33(1-.4) – (30-25) – 10 = $95 million.

Recall that the appropriate discount rates can be determined as follows:

WACC = [Cost of Equity x (Market Value of Equity/Market Value of Equity and Debt)] + [Cost of Debt x (1-Tax Rate) x (Market Value of Debt/Market Value of Equity and Debt)]

To determine the WACC, we first need to determine the cost of equity. This means we must determine the bottom-up beta of the company. The formula for unlevering beta (or to determine what the beta would be in the absence of any debt, used since more debt makes a firm more sensitive to macroeconomic changes) is:

$$\beta_{unlevered} = \frac{\beta_{levered}}{[1+(1\text{-tax rate})(\text{Market Debt/Equity Ratio})]}$$

To re-lever beta, the formula is:

$$\beta_{levered} = \beta_{unlevered}\,[1+((1\text{-tax rate})(\text{Market Debt/Equity Ratio}))]$$

Since we know the industry's levered beta and D/E, we will first determine the industry's unlevered beta, and then use this beta and relever it using Vault Machine's actual (different) debt/equity ratio.

$$\beta_{\text{unlevered of Industry}} = \frac{1.2}{[1+(1-.4)(.25)]} = 1.0435$$

$$\beta_{\text{levered of Vault Machines}} = 1.0435\ [1+((1-.4)(1/2))] = 1.3566$$

Recall also that Cost of Equity = Appropriate Risk Free Rate + Beta(Equity Risk Premium)

So Vault Machine's COE = 5% + 1.3566 x 4.5%
(We stated previously that we would use 4.5% as the U.S. market's equity risk premium.)
= 11.1047%

So Vault Machine's WACC = [0.111047(2,0000/3,000)] + [0.1(1-.4) x (1,000/3,000)]
= 0.0740 + 0.02
= 9.4%

Now we are ready to plug all of the variables into our valuation formula. In this case:

$$\text{Value} = \sum_{t=1}^{t=n} \frac{CF_t}{(1+WACC)^t}$$

Since Vault Machines is expected to grow forever at the same rate, we can simplify the process and value the cash flows like a perpetuity:

Value of the firm = $95 million/((9.4%-5%) = $2.159 billion. Since we know the market is valuing the debt at $1 billion, we subtract this amount out and divide the remainder by 100 million shares outstanding. The firm should be trading at $11.59 a share, not $20 (by this simple analysis.) So it is trading above fair valuation. In real life, the company's growth might actually have been expected to accelerate in the future, and thus our one-stage model might have provided too low a valuation. Using a 2-stage or 3-stage model would require a great deal more work if done by hand, and thus would entail the use of an Excel spreadsheet.

Another common method used to value the equity portion of a company is called relative valuation (or using "comparables"). If you needed to sell your car or home, you might look at what similar cars or homes sold for. Similarly, many analysts compare the value of a stock to the market values of comparable stocks using ratios such as price to earnings and enterprise value to EBITDA. We'll use a valuation of GM during the summer of 2002 using this method to illustrate:

Company	P/E	Price to Book	P/E Forward	Price	EPS Forward
DaimlerChrysler AG	11.62x	1.20x	22.15x	$47.62	$2.15
Fiat S.p.A	8.13x	0.53x	27.51x	$12.38	$0.45
Ford Motor Company	NA	4.35x	77.14x	$16.97	$0.22
Honda Motor Co., Ltd.	7.14x	1.03x	15.61x	$21.54	$1.38
Nissan Motor Co., Ltd.	11.29x	NA	11.27x	$14.43	$1.28
Toyota Motor Corporation	NA	1.69x	20.74x	$53.52	$2.58
Average	7.64x	1.76x	29.07x		
General Motors	33.14x	1.70x	10.80x	$59.07	$5.47

AT $59.07 GM appears to be overvalued using P/E as proxy. Since GM made $1.84 in the trailing twelve months, it should be trading at 7.64 times this amount or $14.06 a share. Analysts often use forward P/E ratios instead. In this case, GM's estimated forward EPS times the average forward P/E would lead to a predicted price of $159.01, meaning that GM is undervalued. Using price to book as a proxy, the firm looks closer to fair value. GM's book value per share at this time was $34.93. Multiplied by 1.76, this gives us a value of $61.48 per share.

As you can see, this is an inexact method. One area of the analysis that is not straightforward is which firms to use as comparables: here we could have added BMW or Renault, but GM at the time of this analysis owned Hughes Electronics, while DaimlerChrysler owned a portion of a defense/aerospace company. Are these two really the same as the other peers that had no holdings in the defense industry? Also, Ford and Nissan were at the time of this analysis experiencing troubles, had no earnings, and their forward earnings were significantly lower than the rest of the groups'; should they therefore be left off of this list?

An analyst needs to make judgment calls on these sorts of issues – there is no one correct answer. Another factor that might make a difference in this case is the fact that firms with higher growth rates generally have higher P/Es than those with lower growth rates. We do not have the various growth rates in this example.

It should be noted that different sector analysts use different multiples. The chart below details multiples commonly used by various industries.

Characteristics of Company	Multiple	Note
Cyclical Manufacturing	P/E and P/E Relative to the Market	Analysts often normalize earnings to take cyclicality into account
High Tech, High Growth	PEG (P/E over Growth Rate in Earnings)	Used because there are often large differences in growth rates
High Growth Industries with No Earnings	P/S (Market Cap over Total Revenues), V/S (Market Cap + Market Value of Debt-Cash over Total Revenues)	This assumes that margins will improve in the future
Heavy Infrastructure	V/EBITDA (Market Cap + Market Value of Debt-Cash over Earnings Before Interest, Taxes Depreciation and Amortization)	This applies to companies in sectors that generally see losses in early years while earnings differ because of differing depreciation methods
REITs	Price/Cash Flow	Usually, there are no capital expenditures from equity earnings
Financial Services	P/BV	The book value of equity is regularly marked to market
Retailing (if D/E levels are similar)	PS	
Retailing (if D/E levels vary widely)	VS	

Finally, analysts sometimes use option theory to value a stock. Real Option valuation holds that the company has the option to delay making an investment, to adjust or alter production as prices changes, to expand production if things seem to be going well, or to abandon projects if they are not worth something. For example, an oil company may have a DCF-based valuation of $10 billion, but a market cap of $20 billion. The extra value may come from the fact the company has unused or underutilized oil reserves that can be tapped should oil prices increase; the firm has the option to expand.

In this case, real option valuation using the Black-Scholes method may be appropriate. Recall that the equation (including dividends) is:

$$C \text{ (call)} = Se\text{-}ytN(d_1) - Ke\text{-}rtN(d_2)$$

$$P \text{ (put)} = Ke\text{-}rt[1\text{-}N(d_2)]\text{-} Se\text{-}yt[1\text{-}N(d_1)]$$

When

$$y \text{ (yield)} = \text{annual dividend/price of the asset}$$

and

$$d_1 = \frac{\ln(S/K)+(r+\sigma^2/2)t}{\sigma\sqrt{t}}$$

$$d_2 = d_1 - \sigma\sqrt{t}$$

where

> S = Current price of the underlying asset (stock or otherwise)
>
> K = Strike price of the option (sometimes called "X" for exercise price instead)
>
> t = Time until the option expires
>
> r = Riskless interest rate (should be for time period closest to lifespan of option)
>
> σ^2 = Variance
>
> D = Dividend yield

In the case of an American oil company with untapped reserves, the probable inputs would be:

> S = Total value of the developed reserves discounted back over the time development takes at the dividend rate (D below)
>
> K = Present value of development cost (discounted at the firm's WACC)
>
> t = The weighted average time until the option to develop these oil reserves expires
>
> r = The appropriate riskless interest rate (if the oil reserve rights last 5 years, the 5-year U.S. Treasury rate, for example.)
>
> σ^2 = The variance in oil prices over the recent past (which could also be the implied volatility of prices based on oil futures.)
>
> D = Net oil production revenue from reserves / value of reserves

As a banker or internal finance professional working on such valuations, you would add the option value of oil reserves to the DCF valuation estimate to come up with the total firm value. This technique is also used to value patents for pharmaceutical, biotech or technology companies, among other things, and can often explain why DCF valuations fall far short of the stock's assigned market price.

8. What does liquidity allow an investor?

Liquidity allows an investor to move in and out of an asset class quickly, enabling one to capitalize on any upside or quickly get out to avoid downside. All else being equal, one can get a better price for a more liquid asset since there is less risk of not being able to sell it. For example, assuming you needed $100,000 cash immediately, would you rather have to sell $100,000 (nominal market value) in Disney stock or $100,000 in (nominal market value) baseball cards?

9. If you worked for the finance division of our company, how would you decide whether or not to invest in a project?

Investing in a project could mean entering a new area of business, buying another company, expanding or broadening an existing business, or changing the way a business is run. The basic test is: will this project earn more money than it will cost from this point forward?

There are several common methods for determining this. One accounting-based method is to compare the firm's cost of capital versus the projects after-tax return on capital. If the projected ROC is higher than the after-tax COC, the project is a good one. (The firm's WACC does not necessarily equal the project's COC; a company with a low debt rating might obtain better interest rates for a relatively less risky project if the loan or bond payments are directly tied to the cash flows generated by the project.) If the project will be funded entirely by equity, one would similarly compare the projected ROE to the COE. Another method measures the "Economic Value Added" or EVA of a project. EVA = (ROC-COC)(Capital Invested in Project). Equity EVA = (ROE-COE)(Equity Invested in Project). A positive estimated EVA means that the project is a good one.

Two cash flow-based measures of investment return use the net present value (NPV) or the internal rate of return (IRR) to determine the merits of a project. Determining the NPV of a project is the sum of the present values of all cash flows less any initial investments, excluding sunk costs. This last distinction is key – sunk costs should not be taken into account. For example, what if you just spent $500 painting half of your car only to find that it will only increase your resale value by $750. You might think that something that costs $1,000 but nets you only $750 is a bad investment; had you known this before starting the paint job you never would have begun. But from this point on, you will probably earn

$0 extra dollars for selling a half painted car, versus netting an extra $250 if you have the job completed. Similarly, only incremental cash flows should be taken into account when deciding on investing in a project.

Determining a project's NPV is essentially the same as valuing a company or a bond:

$$\text{NPV of Project} = \sum_{t=1}^{t=n} \frac{CF_t}{(1+r)^t} - (\text{Initial Investment})$$

Where CF_t = the cash flow in period t, r = discount rate (either COC or COE) and t = the life of the project.

One may argue that any positive NPV, even if it is only $1, is good for a company, since it can only make the company richer. In practice, however, since companies have only a limited amount of money to invest, the project or combination of projects that generate the highest possible NPV are the best, all else being equal.

The IRR (internal rate of return) is the discounted cash flow equivalent of accounting rates of return (like ROC or ROE). The IRR of a project is the discount rate that makes the NPV of a project zero. For example, let us say you invested $1,000,000 in a factory that earned $300,000, $400,000 and $500,000 in years one, two and three respectively. You then sold the factory for $600,000 in year four. At a 24.89% discount rate, the NPV of this project would be zero. Hence, the IRR of this project is 24.89%. If the company can raise money for less than the IRR, than the project is a good one using this measure. Think of it this way: you wouldn't buy a bank CD that earns 5% if the only way you could finance it was through a cash advance on a credit card charging 10%. The chart below summarizes this analysis:

Method Used	It's a Good Project If...	It's a Bad Project If...
Accounting: COC & ROC	After Tax ROC > COC	After Tax ROC < COC
Accounting: COE & ROE	ROE > COE	ROE < COE
Accounting: EVA	EVA > 0	EVA < 0
Accounting: Equity EVA	Equity EVA > 0	Equity EVA < 0
Cash Flow: NPV	NPV > 0	NPV < 0
Cash Flow: IRR	IRR > COC	After Tax ROC < COC
Cash Flow: Equity-Based IRR	IRR > COE	IRR < COE

Which method is best? In general, the cash flow-based methods are more in vogue, since accounting returns are not always the best measure of financial performance. IRR and NPV tend to lead to the same investment decisions, but anomalies do sometimes arise. For example, you may run into situations where your calculations yield more than one IRR. In these cases, it is easier to use NPV. In other cases, IRR and NPV calculations may lead to different investment recommendations when deciding between more than one mutually exclusive project of greatly different size. A larger project might look better on an IRR basis, but worse from an NPV point of view. One way to solve for this is to look at the profitability index (PI), which is NPV/Initial Investment. A higher PI means a better project or set of projects. If the conflict between what IRR and NPV calculations yield cannot be resolved, it is best to favor NPV.

10. How does the yield curve work? What does it mean when it is upward sloping?

This is more likely to come up in a fixed income research or sales and trading interview, but do not be surprised of it is asked in a banking interview (just to test your knowledge). The "yield curve" generally refers to points on a price/time to maturity graph of various U.S. Treasury securities. While yields to maturity on bonds of different maturities are often similar, yields generally do differ. Shorter maturity bonds tend to offer lower yields to maturity while longer-term bonds tend to offer higher ones. This is shown graphically as the yield curve, which sometimes called "the term structure of interest rates." There are a few reasons why yields may differ as maturities change. One theory is the "expectations theory," which states that the slope of the yield curve is determined by expectations of changes in short-term rates. Higher yields on longer-term bonds reflect a belief that rates while increase in the future. If the curve is downward sloping, this theory holds that rates will fall (probably because the economy is slowing, easing fears of inflation and raising the expectation that rates will fall in tandem). If the curve falls then rises again, it may signal that rates will go down temporarily then rise again (perhaps because of monetary easing by the Fed due to an economic slowdown). If the yield is upward sloping, the economy is expected to do well in the future. A sharply rising curve suggests a boom.

Another supposition is the "liquidity preference theory." This theory states that since shorter-term bonds tend to be more liquid than longer-term ones, investors are more willing to hold shorter-term bonds even though they do not pay relatively high yields. A third hypothesis is the "market segmentation" or "preferred habitat" theory, which states that long- and short-term bonds trade differently because different types of investors seek to purchase each an ongoing basis. It is likely that all of these theories are true and work in tandem.

> ## 11. Tell me how you would go about valuing a privately held construction company?

Valuing a private company is essentially no different than valuing a publicly held company (see the earlier question on valuing a company or stock): one uses some combination of DCF, relative ("comparable") and option valuation techniques for any type of firm. (Remember, however, that relative valuation and the FCFE or DDM methods of DCF valuation should only be used to value the firm's equity, not the firm as whole.) For a DCF valuation, whether or not to use a one, two or three-stage valuation depends on the market the company is in and the macroeconomic environment. A home building company in Las Vegas operating during an economic boom will likely have two or three stages of growth, whereas a firm specializing in erecting steel plants in the Northeast U.S. might only grow at one steady rate.

There are differences in the details when it comes to valuing a private company in any industry, however. These differences arise mainly when it comes to DCF valuation. When it comes to relative valuation, one would follow the same steps as outlined in the answer to the valuing a stock question. For a construction company, using the P/E multiples of publicly traded peers is probably the best choice. Real option valuation might be appropriate if the company has the exclusive right to build potentially valuable properties. If so, the only difference between a public and a private company using real options lies in the determination of the weighted average cost of capital (WACC).

For a DCF valuation, the determination of the cost of equity (COE) or the WACC will also differ. Remember, the WACC is based partly on the COE. The cost of equity estimation usually depends on either a historical regression beta (found on Bloomberg among other data sources) or a bottom-up beta estimation. Since no historical regression betas are available (private companies do not trade), one must perform a bottom-up beta estimation using an average of the regression betas of similarly sized publicly traded peers as a proxy. In this case, one would look at similar-sized construction companies (as we did in the earlier question).

Recall:

$$\beta_{unlevered} = \frac{\beta_{levered}}{[1+(1\text{-tax rate})(\text{Market Debt/Equity Ratio})]}$$

To re-lever beta, the formula is:

$$\beta_{levered} = \beta_{unlevered}\,[1+((1\text{-tax rate})(\text{Market Debt/Equity Ratio}))]$$

In the worst-case scenario, where the firm either has no good peers or is too small to compare to publicly traded companies, one might resort to using a so-called "accounting-based" beta. This is done as follows: First, one would determine the quarterly accounting earnings for the private company as far back as records go. If no quarterly records are available, one should use semi-annual numbers and if these are not available, annual numbers. Second, one should regress these accounting earnings against changes in a market-wide index (like the S&P 500 or Wilshire Total Market) over the same time period. Third, one must determine the slope of the regression generated using these inputs. This slope is the "accounting-based" beta. This approach is problematic since there will be far fewer observations than there would be for a normal publicly traded company's regression beta. Also, accountants tend to smooth earnings. This approach should only be used as a last resort.

To determine the cost of debt (and its relative weight) for WACC, one can take the borrowing rate of any very recent bank loans and assume that all debt on the books should be valued (like a bond) using this rate. If the debt is all very different or there are no recent loans, one might estimate what the bond rating for the firm should be given the assigned ratings of firms of similar size and with similar financial ratio values (such as EBITDA/Debt Expense, also called the interest coverage ratio). Using the interest rate assigned to companies with such a rating, one would value all of the debt on the books like a bond.

If one is valuing the company as an acquisition target, one might add the additional step of estimating the COE or WACC based on what it would be once the firm becomes part of the acquiring firm; the WACCs should converge to a weighted average. If the acquirer is many times larger than the construction company in question and has a much lower WACC, this could substantially raise the construction company's eventual valuation. Even if the firm is not being valued for a potential acquisition, one might add the step of gradually moving the firm towards the D/E ratio of its peer group if it is currently far out of line, thus gradually adjusting the WACC as well.

$$\beta_{private\ firm} = \beta_{unlevered}\ [1+((1\text{-tax rate})(\text{Industry Average Debt/Equity Ratio}))]$$

Once one has determined the WACC, there are a few more issues one must take into account when valuing a privately held firm. First, private firms may have a shorter history than most publicly traded firms, in which case more extrapolation is required when making future cash flow projections. Second, private firms often use accounting techniques that would not be acceptable for public companies. Third, many private companies (especially "mom and pop" businesses) list what would otherwise be personal expenses as business expenses. Fourth, and similarly, owner/operators pay themselves salaries and may also pay themselves dividends. Past numbers may therefore have to be adjusted to show what they would have been had the firm been public; this is true both for relative valuation and the DCF valuation of a private company slated to go public or be purchased by a public firm. Future cash flow may have to also be adjusted to reflect the expense of salaried employees replacing owner/operators.

It is important to note that in both DCF and relative valuation, it makes a difference as to why one is valuing a company. If the company intends to stay private or is being priced for sale to another private company, the valuation will likely be lower than if it is to be sold to a publicly traded company or if it is planning an IPO. First, private businesses cannot be bought and sold as easily as a public one; thus one must estimate an illiquidity discount for a private firm to remain in private hands. As a shortcut many bankers lower the valuation by 20% (this is what past studies have shown the average discount to be) and then arbitrarily adjust this percentage upwards or downwards depending on the size of the firm in question. (Surely, multi-billion dollar private companies like Hallmark or Cargill would have a lower illiquidity discount than a local construction company.)

Second, once the beta has been determined, it may need to be adjusted upwards further since the beta estimation of a publicly traded firm is a measure of market risk, and assumes that the firm's stockholders are well diversified. Private firm owners tend to have a large portion if not the majority of their wealth tied up in a business. In this case, if the construction firm is being valued for purchase by another private company (or is not going to be purchased at all), the beta should reflect the increased risk associated with this lack of diversification. This is done as follows:

Total Beta = Preliminary Beta / Firm's Correlation with Market.

This is why it is generally preferable for the owners of a private company seeking to liquidate their holdings to go public or be purchased by a publicly traded company rather than be bought by another private firm; being public generally means a lower COE and thus a higher valuation.

12. Why might a technology company be more highly valued in the market in terms of P/E than a steel company stock?

You may recall from the question on how to value a stock that relative P/E is affected by the growth rate in earnings. Generally speaking, higher growth companies (and industries) have higher P/E ratios than lower growth ones. Mathematically this can be shown by breaking down the components of the ratio into their equity DCF components:

Using the DDM model:

P = Dividends per Share/$(r-g)$.

Dividing both sides by EPS:

P/E = (Payout Ratio)$(1+g)/(r-g)$

Using the FCFE method of valuation:

P = FCFE/$(r-g)$, and
P/E = (FCFE/Earnings)$(1+g)/(r-g)$

All else being equal, higher growth ("g" in the equation) means higher P/E ratios. One can safely assume that technology companies (even in the down market of 2002) will grow faster than steel companies.

13. When should a company raise money via equity? When should a company raise funds using debt?

As you may recall:

Cost of Equity = Appropriate Risk Free Rate + Beta (Equity Risk Premium)

Only very low Beta companies will have a cost of equity that approaches their cost of debt, but in most cases debt is cheaper than equity from a firm's point of view. (Issuing stock is not "free," since it dilutes the ownership stakes of the firm's existing owners.) However, coupon-bearing debt requires regular payments. Therefore, younger and smaller firms with good growth prospects but more volatile cash flows are better suited for equity, while mature companies or those with steady cash flows tend to use more debt. Even zero-coupon debt, which requires only a balloon payment at maturity, is only appropriate for firms that have fairly certain future large cash flows.

Some would argue that a company might want to use equity (such as when making an acquisition) in cases where management believes its own stock to be very highly (or even over) valued; thus AOL used stock to buy Time Warner and many dot-coms sold stock before March 2000 even though they did not need the funds. In other cases, existing bank or debt covenants may require a certain debt/equity ratio or cash balance, in which case a mature company with too much debt may issue stock to keep within its agreements.

14. How would one price the different elements of a convertible bond?

Although this question often pops up in sales and trading interviews, many banks staff convertible bond capital markets/origination employees with bankers, so this question sometimes comes up in corporate finance interviews. In addition, as a banker you may need to discuss potential convertible offerings with a CFO; as an internal corporate finance professional you may help to decide whether your firm should raise money via equity, debt or hybrid securities like convertibles.

First, the textbook definition of a convertible bond: A convertible bond is a bond that gives bondholders the option, but not the obligation, to convert into a certain number of shares. This option is usually triggered if the bond issuer's stock hits a certain, higher price in the future. Conversion becomes more likely as the underlying stock price increases. Firms normally use convertibles to lower the interest payments, when all else equal, the right to convert into equity gives the bond more value. From a trading standpoint, a convertible bond behaves at different times like:

A bond. When it is "deep out of the money" (the underlying stock price is far below the conversion level) the overwhelming majority of the value comes from the interest payments;

An option. Since the option to convert is no different than that of a traditional stock option, traditional option valuation techniques can be used;

Straight equity. When the convertible is deep in the money (or the issuer's stock far above the conversion price) it becomes a near certainty that the bondholder will exercise his or her right to exercise.

For valuation purposes, a convertible can be broken down into a straight bond and a conversion option. To value the bond component, take the coupon (face value interest) rate on the convertible bond and compare it to the interest rate that the company would have had to pay if it had issued a straight bond. This should be what the company pays on similar outstanding issues. If the company has no bonds outstanding, one can infer from its bond rating what the company might pay. Using the maturity, coupon rate and the market interest rate of the convertible bond, one can estimate the value of the bond as the sum of the present value of the coupons at the market interest rate and the present value of the face value of the bond at the market interest rate. Whatever is left over is the equity portion.

If it were a convertible offering yet to be issued, one would estimate the price of the call options imbedded in the convertible issue (using the option pricing methods discussed in a previous question) and subtract this amount from what the value of an ordinary bond of an equal maturity and face value would be. To determine the interest rate the issuer would then need to pay, one would find the rate, which when plugged into the bond pricing equation, is equal to this new amount (ordinary bond less option value).

15. How would you value a non-U.S. company?

Valuing a foreign company involves the same steps as outlined in the question on how to value a company or stock. As with the question on valuing a private company, it is the small details that make such a valuation different.

When employing relative valuation, one should use local companies as peers whenever possible. Thus one would compare small German banks on a price to book basis using other German banks (or if need be, other E.U.-based banks.) In certain cases, there are no local peers (Nokia is the only Finnish mobile phone manufacturer) or there are only a few players who operate globally (such as in the auto industry).

In such cases, using international peers is appropriate, though one must keep in mind local difference that may account for inconsistent ratio levels between companies. For example, if one compared, say South African Breweries with Heineken and Anheuser-Busch on a P/E or V/EBITDA basis in 2002, one must take into the account SAB's greater exposure to emerging markets, which (all else being equal) might increase the firm's risk and thus lower its relative valuation. Even in two markets of similar risk, different factors might affect what might otherwise be a clean comparison. For example, according to the Dividend Discount Method of Valuation:

$$P = DPS/(r-g).$$

If we divide both sides by EPS, one gets:

$$P/E = \text{Payout Ratio}(1+g)/(r-g)$$

Using the FCFE method of valuation:

$$P = FCFE/(r-g), \text{ and}$$
$$P/E = (FCFE/\text{Earnings})(1+g)/(r-g)$$

All else being equal, lower interest means lower discount rates and thus also higher P/E ratios. Japanese companies tend to have higher P/Es than their European counterparts because of Japan's relatively low rates. When comparing peers of or from different countries, such subtle differences can affect a valuation greatly. Finally, while many large non-U.S. companies like Sony and DaimlerChrysler report using U.S. accounting standards, many more do not. One should therefore make certain to adjust for any accounting differences between the U.S. and the company in question's home country.

If one utilizes real options in a non-U.S. company valuation, remember that three of the inputs are:

K = (Exercise or Strike Price) = Present value of development cost (discounted at the firm's WACC).

r = The appropriate riskless interest rate (if the oil reserve rights last 5 years, the 5-year U.S. Treasury rate, for example).

σ^2 = The variance in asset price.

Each of these variables may be different for a non-U.S. company. "K" will differ if the WACC is different (more on this as we discuss using DCF in pricing a foreign company). The riskless rate will almost certainly be different than a similar maturity U.S. Treasury security. And the variance may depend upon the volatility of similar assets in the firm's local market, which will likely differ from the volatility of such assets in the U.S. "S", "t" and "D" (strike price, time and dividend yield) are not affected.

When it comes to using DCF methods, one should make certain to adjust for any accounting differences between the U.S. and the company in question's home country when looking at past numbers or making forward financial estimates. One must use the appropriate currency for all calculations. Thus, a Mexican company should be valued in Pesos throughout while the Mexican risk-free rate should be used. Once a value has been determined, this can be translated into dollar terms. Nominal amounts should be used unless the company is in a very high inflation environment; only then should one compute all numbers using "real" or "constant" (inflation-neutral) terms.

For non-U.S. companies' cost of debt, one would use whatever cost of debt is appropriate given the firm's bond rating. If there is no rating available, one should estimate one and adjust the WACC by adding a risk premium. Without a rating, the cost of and relative weight of debt can be calculated using the firm's financial characteristics and/or interest expenses, just as with a U.S. firm. If the company is in a country with a lower debt rating than the U.S., one would generally then add the difference between where sovereign debt trades in the company's home country and the U.S. For example, let us take a Southeast Asian real estate company in an emerging market country where 10-year government bonds trade at, say 10.1% versus 5.1% in the U.S. Thus the so-called "Default Spread" would be 5%. If this Southeast Asian real estate company had an S&P, Moody's or Fitch-assigned rating, one would use the cost of debt appropriate for companies with this rating. If not, one would look at what similar firms in the U.S. had as a cost of debt and add the default spread. If companies in the U.S. with similar interest coverage ratios can borrow at 9%, we should assume that the real estate company could borrow at no better then 14%.

The COE would also differ. There are several prevalent methods for determining by how much. One (and probably the easiest) way to do this is called the "Bond Rating" method. Since sovereign bond rating by S&P, Moody's and Fitch take into account country risk, one assumes that:

The country risk premium = Risk Premium$_{US}$+ (Default Spread on Sovereign Bonds)

The equity risk premium would be equal to or higher than in the U.S. using this approach. For example, the bonds of a country like the U.K. or France would trade at the same interest rate as U.S. Treasuries, so using this method the risk premium would still be 4.5% (again, this is number we are using for convenience). For an emerging market country with a 5% default spread, the appropriate equity risk premium would be 4.5% + 5% = 9.5%, which would significantly increase the COE and thus the WACC, all else being equal.

Another method is the "Relative Equity Market" method. Since certain equity markets are more or less volatile than the U.S., this method assumes that:

The country risk premium = Equity Risk Premium$_{US}$ (σCountry Equity/σUS Equity)

As you may recall:

Cost of Equity = Appropriate (Local) Risk-Free Rate + Beta(Equity Risk Premium)

A non-U.S. company will likely have a different risk-free rate and beta (although for large companies in small markets, like Nortel in 2000 vis-à-vis Canada, one might substitute the S&P and thus use the same market to calculate beta). The equity risk premium would be higher for more volatile markets and lower for less volatile one using this approach. The equity risk premium would also be higher for companies in non AAA-rated countries.

A third method is to use the "Bond Method" in conjunction with equity market volatility. Here one assumes that:

The country risk premium = Risk Premium$_{US}$[(σMost Comprehensive Local Equity Index)/(σLocal Government Long-Term Bond)]

A fourth method involves predicting the implied equity premium of a market. This is a rather complicated method, but in a nutshell it assumes that:

Total Value of All Stocks = (Dividends and Stock Buybacks Expected Next Year)/(Required Returns on Stocks - Expected Growth Rate)

We can use a local index as a proxy for the "Total Value of All Stocks." We can use analysts' estimates for what dividends on all stocks in the local index will be for "Dividends", and analysts' growth estimate for "Growth." It is then algebraically possible to extract the expected return on stocks. By subtracting out the local risk-free rate, one can find equity risk premium. Since most stock markets are made up of companies that will grow in one, two or three stages, in reality the calculations are much more complicated.

No matter which of these methods for determining WACC one chooses, one should take into account what proportion of a firm's revenues and operations are actually located in their headquarter country. For example, Cemex, a large Mexican cement manufacturer, gets a large percentage of its revenue from and has many of its factories in Europe and the U.S. Many South African firms are listed on the London Stock Exchange and have moved their headquarters to London, but have most of their operations in and derive most of their revenue from Africa. UBS, Roche, and Nestlé are clearly more than just Swiss companies. In these sorts of cases, one may want to weigh the COE proportionately based on the origin of cash flows and the location of the firm's operations.

16. What is operating leverage?

Operating leverage refers to percentage of costs that are fixed versus variable. An airline, manufacturing or hotel company with lots of long-term property leases and unionized employees must make lease and salary payments whether sales rise or fall. On the other extreme, a consulting firm that has many employees working on site with clients or a technology company with high R&D expenditures might have the flexibility to lay-off employees or lower R&D expenses should sales falter, or to increase employees or spending more if sales rise. On the other hand, firms with high degrees of operating leverage generally experience significant increases in operating income as sales increase. A firm's degree of operating leverage is defined as:

DOL = 1+(fixed costs/profits) = % change in profits/% change in sales.

> **17. Your client wants to buy one of two banks. One is trading at a 12x P/E, and the other trades at a 16x P/E. Which should your client try to buy? Do you even have enough information to determine this?**

There are two ways in which this question is tricky. First, P/E is usually analyzed in relation to expected future growth in earnings. Higher growth companies tend to have higher P/Es, all else being equal. Since we do not know the banks' growth rates, we cannot say for certain. Second, in the answer in an earlier question we stated that price to book is a better measure of relative value for the financial services industry, since the book value of equity is regularly marked to market at banks, brokerages and insurance companies. Therefore, we couldn't make as good a guess as possible even if the growth rates were known. Return on equity is the variable which best matches P/BV. Mathematically this can also be shown as follows:

According to the dividend discount model,

P = Dividend per Share/(discount rate – growth in earnings)

Also, return on equity (ROE) = EPS / Book Value of Equity, and by combining these two formulas the value of equity is:

$$P = \frac{BV(ROE)(Payout\ Ratio)(1 + g)}{(r\text{-}g)}$$

or

$$P/BV = \frac{ROE(Payout\ Ratio)(1+g)}{(r\text{-}g)}$$

or

Growth = (1 - Payout ratio)ROE

Either way, higher returns on equity mean higher growth rates and also a higher P/BV and thus a higher valuation for the financial services firm in question, all else being equal.

18. What are some ways to determine if a company might be a credit risk?

The easiest method, of course, is to look at what the rating agencies (S&P, Moody's, and/or Fitch) say about a company; it is their job to analyze such risk. These ratings may be unavailable, however, or you may wish to do further due diligence.

There are several potential sources of risk any company faces. When analyzing the credit risk of a potential recipient of financing, one should examine all of these from a subjective standpoint. There are international-related risks (host government changes in law, political unrest, currency risk); domestic risks (recession, inflation or deflation, interest rate risk, demographic shifts, political and regulatory risk); industry risk (technological change, increased competition, increasing supply costs, unionization); and company-specific risk (management (in)competence, strategic outlook, legal action). Additionally, one must objectively look for signs that any subjectively determined risk scenarios will affect the finances of a company. Short-term liquidity risk can be analyzed by looking at some of the following accounting equations:

Current Ratio = Current Assets/Current Liabilities

This ratio has been moving below 2 for most U.S. companies, and some industries average below 1. Generally, it is somewhere between 1 and 2. The lower this number is moving, the better the firm is at managing inventory. A sharp rise either means an expected boom in business or an overstocked warehouse.

Quick Ratio = (Cash + Marketable Securities + Receivables)/Current Liabilities

In some industries, where inventory can be quickly liquidated,

Quick Ratio = (Cash + Marketable Securities + Receivables + Inventory)/Current Liabilities

Quick ratios are usually around 0.5 – 1.0. The higher the number, the faster a company can pay debt in a worse case scenario. An increasing quick ratio may also mean that the company is not managing inventory or receivables as well as it could.

Other short-term measurements (the norms of which vary from industry to industry) are:

Operating Cash Flow (CFO) to Current Liabilities (CL) = CFO/Average CL

Accounts Receivable (AR) Turnover = Sales/Average AR

Inventory Turnover = Cost of Goods Sold/Average Inventories

Accounts Payable Turnover = Purchases/Average Accounts Payable

If the company in question is far from its industry's norm for such ratios, it may be a short-term credit risk. A company might be a short-term credit risk but a safe bet longer-term (or vice-versa). Accounting ratios used to determine longer-term risk include:

Long-Term Debt Ratio = Long-Term Debt/(Long-Term Debt + Shareholders Equity)

Debt/Equity Ratio = Long-Term Debt/ Shareholders Equity

Liabilities/Assets Ratio = Total Liabilities/Total Assets

Operating Cash Flow to Total Liabilities Ratio = Cash Flow From Continuing Activities/Average Total Liabilities

Operating Cash Flow to Capital Expenditures Ratio = Cash Flow From Continuing Activities/Capital Expenditures

Again, if any of these longer-term ratios are far worse than what they are for the industry as a whole, you may have a longer-term credit risk. The most commonly used long-term risk measure is the Interest Coverage Ratio (ICR) (use this if you have to pick only one):

ICR = EBITDA/Interest Expense

This ratio is less frequently looked at as:

ICR = (Net Income + Interest Expense + Income Tax Expense+ Minority Interest in Earnings)/Interest Expense

For larger U.S. companies, S&P usually assigns its best rating of AAA to firms with an ICR of higher than 8.5; financial services firms must generally have an ICR of above 3 and smaller firms one of above 12.5 to get an AAA rating. Larger firms with an ICR below 2.5, financial services firms with an ICR below .8, and smaller companies with an ICR below 3.5 tend to get a BB or lower rating and thus are classified as not credit-worthy or "junk."

19. How does compounding work? Would I be better off with 10% annually, semi-annually, or daily?

Daily would pay the most. Paid semiannually, $1 invested at rate "r" will grow to $[1+(r/2)]^{2T}$. Paid monthly, $1 invested at rate "r" will grow to $[1+(r/12)]^{12N}$. It can be proven mathematically that the larger number of compounding periods gets, the larger the final value of $100 gets. If one could pay interest every instant, $100 would grow into e^{rt}, when e is approximately 2.71828. To put it another way, your credit card company may charge you 1.5% a month, but you can see that this costs you more per year than 18% (which is why the "A.P.R." is listed is $19.56%). Try it on your calculator and see.

20. What is duration?

All firms expect their bankers to be knowledgeable about bonds (particularly if you are placed in debt capital markets/origination). Remember, most larger corporations issue more debt than equity.

Think of bond payments like children on a seesaw. If a bond pays $10 a year for 29 years, and then paid $400 the 30th and last year, at what point would the present values of these cash flows balance if they were instead children on the see-saw? Duration is this measure.

Duration (An Ilustration)

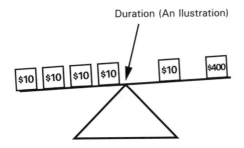

Why is duration important? There two main reasons. First, when bond prices rise or fall, interest rates fall or rise. For small changes in interest rates, the duration of a bond will allow you to figure out how much a bond's price will change. It is a measure of interest rate sensitivity. Second, knowing duration of bond or a portfolio of bonds (or loans) is important in order to match assets with liabilities. A classic example of a failure to do so sparked the Savings and Loan crises in the U.S. in the late 1970's. Banks took in deposits, which were generally withdrawn in well under five years. Meanwhile, they loaned out the same money in the form of 30-year mortgages or invested in long-term U.S. government bonds. When interest rates spiked in the 1970's, S&Ls found themselves paying out double-digit interest on short-term deposits while collecting low single digit interest on bonds and home loans. This was a classic case of "duration mismatch." On a personal level, you may have experienced a time when you were eventually going to receive more money than you owed, but your credit card on other bills were due before your cash inflows arrived; this is a sort of duration mismatch. By computing the duration of ones' portfolio, one can hedge or otherwise structure to help insure that cash inflows match cash outflows.

Classic, or "MacCaulay's Duration," measures the effective maturity of a bond, defined as the weighted average of the times until each payment, with weights proportional to the present value of the payments. Put another way, it is how long on average bondholders will have to wait to get their money back. Mathematically:

$$w_t = \frac{CF_t/(1 + YTM)^t}{P}$$

Where: w = weight and CF_t = Cash flow made at time t

And duration (or D) is:

$$D = \sum_{t=1}^{t=n} tw$$

For example:

YTM = 10%   Coupon = 8% (annually)

P = $1,000   n = 4 years (maturity)

$$\text{Duration} = \frac{\dfrac{80\,(1)}{(1.1)} + \dfrac{80\,(2)}{(1.1)_2} + \dfrac{80\,(3)}{(1.1)^3} + \dfrac{1,080\,(4)}{(1.1)^4}}{\dfrac{80}{(1.1)} + \dfrac{80}{(1.1)^2} + \dfrac{80}{(1.1)^3} + \dfrac{1,080}{(1.1)^4}} = 3.56 \text{ years}$$

Another duration equation assumes that one knows the slope of the price change per change in interest rate of a bond. This formula is written:

$$D = \frac{-(slope)[1+y/2]}{P}$$

Where P = price and y = yield. Alternatively this can be stated as:

$$D = \frac{\delta P/P}{\delta y/(1+y/2)}$$

With $\delta P/P$ being the percentage change in price.

Some more things you may want to remember (believe it or not, some of these things have come up in interviews):

a. The duration of a zero coupon bond equals its time to maturity while duration is always less than maturity for coupon-bearing bonds. Thus a three-year coupon-bearing bond has a lower duration than a three-year zero.

b. Holding the coupon rate constant, a bond's duration and interest rate sensitivity generally increase with time to maturity.

c. The slope of a duration graph is less than one (duration increases by less than a year for each year's increase in maturity). (This statement is true only for coupon bonds. For zero-coupon bonds, duration increases on a one-to-one basis with maturity.)

d. Holding time to maturity and YTM constant, a bond's duration and interest rate sensitivity increases as the coupon rate decreases.

Bonus hard question: **What is the difference between MacCaulay's and modified duration?** (This is an actual question asked in a banking interview.) Answer: Modified duration is the percentage change in price for a change in yield. Mathematically:

$$\text{Modified Duration} = - \frac{\delta P/P}{\delta y}$$

Or

$$\text{Modified Duration} = \frac{\text{Duration}}{(1+y/2)}$$

Where m = compounding frequency per year.

21. What would happen to a company's stock if it announced a large loss due to a write-down of goodwill?

First, what is "goodwill?" When one firm purchases another, the acquiring firm must allocate assets to the new, combined company's balance sheet. Value is assigned to identifiable and tangible assets like land, buildings, and equipment first. Next, value is assigned to identifiable intangible assets like patents, customer lists, or trade names. The remainder is listed on the balance sheet as "goodwill." In short, you can just say goodwill is the difference between the book value of the purchased company and the actual price paid.

Let's say General Electric purchases an advertising company like Omnicom and a brand-driven firm like Coca-Cola. The amount of goodwill left on the balance sheet of the combined company would be much greater than if GE bought General Motors or Equity Office Properties. This is because a relatively larger portion of GM's and Equity Office's value is derived from their ownership of car factories or office buildings. Omnicom derives much of its value from the skills and knowledge of its employees. As much as managers tout "human capital" these days, there is no balance sheet item for the term. Similarly, the majority of Coke's value comes from its brand names and "secret formula" (which is not patented).

U.S. GAAP (Generally Accepted Accounting Principles) used to require firms to amortize goodwill much the same way they depreciate tangible assets. This is no longer required: firms must now "write-down" goodwill only when it becomes "impaired." For example, if after GE purchased Coca-Cola, scientists discovered that orange juice causes cancer, the ability of GE to earn money off the Minute Maid brand name would become impaired. Thus some of the NPV of future income that had been projected to come from the Minute Maid division of Coca Cola/GE would have to be subtracted from goodwill on the balance sheet. This subtraction would also be taken from net income as a one-time loss.

Consequently, if a company announces a big write-down of goodwill, this means that the company no longer expects to earn as much money as it had hoped from the intangible and unidentifiable assets in question. This would lower net income; in the case of AOL Time Warner in 2002 or Nortel in 2001, it could lower accounting earnings by tens of billions. However, this is considered a non-cash charge, since it does not affect actual cash coming into the firm for the quarter the charge is taken. Indeed, it may not affect cash flows for several quarters or even years. If analysts and investors foresee such a charge being taken (which they often do), this massive loss is ignored, and only "operating earnings" are considered. In the case of AOL Time Warner and Nortel, investors had already seen the fortunes of Yahoo!, Lucent, JDS Uniphase, and the like tumble before the announcement of the write-downs. Many dot-coms, technology and telecommunication equipment companies (like JDS Uniphase) had themselves already announced write-downs. The stocks of AOL Time Warner and Nortel were therefore largely unaffected. A firm's stock will only fall if the write-down is completely unexpected, or much larger than expected.

22. What is convexity?

As bond prices rise and fall along with interest rate changes, they do not do so in the linear way assumed by duration. A straight-line approximation is valid for small changes in interest rates. For larger jumps, another measure is needed. Convexity is a second derivative of the price function and measures the actual curvature of the price-yield curve of a bond.

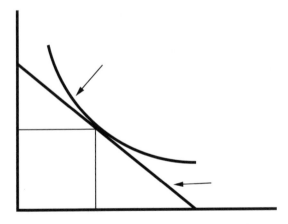

Convexity is generally considered desirable in a bond, since the greater the curvature the more prices will increase when yields decrease and fall less when yields increase. Convexity also assumes that as yields rise, the price-bond curve becomes flatter. Convexity is important because it allows one to improve the duration estimation for changes in bond prices. Mathematically, it can represented as shown below:

$$\sum_{t=1}^{n} \left[CF_t / (1+y)^t (t^2+t) \right]$$

$$\text{Convexity} = \frac{1}{P(1+y)^2}$$

Where n = time until maturity of the bond, CF_t = the cash flow paid to the bondholder at time t, P = price, and y = yield. You will never have to know this equation in an interview, but those of you familiar with calculus might find this equation helpful in understanding convexity.

23. What's deferred tax?

A deferred tax liability is a non-cash balance sheet item stemming from differences between reported accounting income and taxable income. Future tax deductions stemming from similar differences are classified as a deferred tax asset. An example is when a manufacturer of vacuum cleaners increases the estimated number of warranties to be redeemed, due to a defect found in a top selling model. This would immediately lower accounting earnings, but this charge would not be tax-deductible. It would instead create a deferred tax asset since the firm would not be able to deduct the expense for tax purposes until the warranty repairs were actually made.

24. What is securitization?

Securitization is the immediate monetizing of future cash flows. Recall earlier, in our discussion of duration, we said that when interest rates spiked in the 1970's, S&Ls found themselves paying out double-digit interest on short-term deposits while collecting low single digit interest on bonds and home loans. This was a classic case of "duration mismatch." The way out of this mess for many S&Ls was to sell the rights to future mortgage payments (via investment banks) to institutional investors just like bonds (now called CMOs or collateralized mortgage obligations). Since the mortgage-backed bond market was started in the late 1970's, virtually any sort of predictable cash flow that can be securitized has been. Examples include credit card payments, auto loans, student loans, even songwriting royalties ("Bowie Bonds") and several states' tobacco case settlement money. The advantage to the seller of the bond is that it receives cash immediately and mitigates any risk of suffering from future defaults by debtors.

25. Rising U.S. trade deficits are a problem. We need to get our deficit lower. Do you agree?

Rising deficits are not necessarily a problem. After all, Japan had a trade surplus throughout the 1990's while being mired in recession, while the U.S. had the world's strongest economy and high deficits during this time. The trade deficit is defined as follows:

Trade Balance = Exports - Imports of Goods = NX. If the balance is negative, we have a trade deficit.

You should recall from basic economics that

GDP = C + I + G + NX (with C = consumer spending, I = investment, and G = government spending). Lower NX must be offset by higher C, I, or G. In the case of the U.S. during the 90's, C (consumption) and I (investment) were both higher. The total dollars invested in the U.S. economy during this time included massive amounts invested by foreigners. Fast growing economies like the U.S. or the so-called "Asian Tigers" attract foreign investment while having trade deficits. Hence, higher trade deficits are not necessarily a sign of economic weakness but can be a sign of confidence in an economy by global investors (assuming the deficit is financing investment and not consumption or government budget deficits).

26. How do you calculate market capitalization of a company?

Multiply the current stock price by the number of shares outstanding. For example, if MSFT is trading at $52/share and there are 5,415.46 million shares outstanding, the market cap would be calculated as $52/share*5,415.46 million shares = $281,603.9.

27. How do you calculate the market value of a firm?

Total firm value (V) equals the sum of the market value of the firm's debt (D) and equity (E). Or, $V = D + E$.

28. What is the breakup value of a firm?

The breakup value of the firm is determined by analyzing the liquidation value of all tangible assets (A) and liabilities (L). These are netted (i.e., $A - L$) and the result is the residual value accruing to shareholders.

29. How can a company raise its stock price?

There are many ways in which a company could do this. These include:

- Initiation of a large public stock repurchase. This sends a signal to the market that the company feels that its stock is undervalued. This means that the company can't find better investment alternatives than its own stock. Financial ratios such as earnings per share and return on earnings should increase since there are fewer outstanding shares (corporate share repurchases go into the treasury stock account, which is not included in the number of shares outstanding).

- Announcement of planned changes to organizational structure, such as mounting major cost cutting campaign, consolidation or refocusing of product lines, making management changes and so on.

- Structural changes, including mergers, acquisitions and divestitures.

- Announcing an increase in dividends. Since the share price should be valued as the DCF of future expected cash flows, if cash flows increase, the share price should increase.

30. What are some reasons companies carry out mergers?

A merger occurs when two companies agree to combine operations and go forward as a single company. The assets and liabilities of the two companies are combined. They can occur for a variety of reasons. Benefits can include cost reduction, economies of scale or the ability to enter a new market to exploit new opportunities at a lower cost than would be possible without the merger. There are different kinds of mergers as well.

• **Horizontal merger:** a merger that takes place between two competitors (companies in the same line of business), such as one airline purchasing another. The Daimler-Chrysler merger is an example. Horizontal mergers can result in industry consolidation. If industry competition is sufficiently diluted after the horizontal merger, the new company may be able to raise prices and keep them high. For example, the Federal Trade Commission reports that had the merger between Staples (an office supply store) and Office Depot been allowed to go through, Staples would have been the only office supply store in many areas, and would have been able to raise prices 13 percent.

• **Vertical merger:** a merger of non-competing companies, where one makes a component needed by the other. These firms have a buyer-seller relationship. Example: Time-Warner's merger with Turner Broadcasting Systems. Vertical mergers can increase barriers to entry by either refusing to sell needed production inputs to competitors or raising their prices. These types of mergers can also result in lowered prices that competitors cannot match, synergies in product design, and more efficient use of resources.

• **Conglomerate merger:** a combination between companies in unrelated businesses. Goals of conglomerate mergers can include diversification. The theory: the companies are worth more together than separately. Conglomerates have fallen out of favor in recent years; investors today prefer to diversity portfolios, not purchase diversified companies. Divestitures and breakups of huge conglomerates built during the 1960s and 1970s are now common.

31. What is an acquisition?

An acquisition is where one company (the acquiring firm) seeks to gain control over another (the target). An acquisition may be the cheapest way to buy desired assets or gain entry into a particular field. The takeover may be friendly or hostile. In a friendly takeover, the acquiring firm makes an offer to the target firm's management and board of directors to establish either a parent-subsidiary relationship, a merger or a consolidation of the two firms. In a hostile takeover, the acquiring firm proceeds against the wishes of the management/board, normally by accumulating stock and making tender offers directly to the shareholders.

32. What are some of the defensive tactics that a target firm may employ to block a hostile takeover?

There are a variety of strategies a target firm may employ, many designed to make the takeover economically unattractive to the target.

- **Changing the bylaws of the corporation** — for example, by implementing a staggered board so that only 1/3 of the directors are elected each year and/or requiring a supermajority (for example, 75%) to approve a merger or acquisition.

- **Poison pill shareholder rights plan** — the target company uses this tactic to make its stock less attractive to the potential acquirer. According to the Delaware Supreme Court, "A poison pill is a defensive mechanism adopted by corporations that wish to prevent unwanted takeovers. Upon the occurrence of certain 'triggering' events, such as a would-be acquirer's purchase of a certain percentage of the target corporation's shares, or the announcement of a tender offer, all existing shareholders, except for the would-be acquirer, get the right to purchase debt or stock of the target at a discount. This action dilutes the would-be acquirer's stake in the company and increases the costs of acquisition."

- **Golden parachutes** — lucrative benefits, such as stock options, severance pay and so on, given to top management in the event of hostile takeovers. Not only does this increase the cost of the merger, but also results in loss of talented managers and other employees, who may be assets coveted by the acquirer.

- **Employee Stock Option Plan (ESOP)** — allows lower-level employees to purchase shares and appoint trustees who will (presumably) support management in a defense against a hostile takeover.

- **Shareholder Stock Purchase Program (SSPP)** — a program allowing shareholders to purchase additional shares at a low price should a triggering event occur. The triggering event can be, for example, whenever an outside entity acquires more than 20% of the stock.

- **Defensive litigation** — seek help from the Justice Department on the grounds that the merger will be anti-competitive.

- **White knight** — another acquirer more acceptable to management.

---

33. Who is Alan Greenspan and why is he followed so closely by the press? How will the stock market be affected if he announces an increase in interest rates?

Alan Greenspan is the Chairman of the Federal Reserve Board. He is closely followed by the press because the Federal Reserve Board has a number of tools it can use to stimulate or slow economic growth.

One of these tools is the ability to alter the interest rate charged between banks for overnight loans. This discount rate is widely used as a benchmark against which other rates are compared. The effect of a rise in interest rates depends on whether the announced increase was anticipated or not. If the markets anticipate a rate increase of 50bp (50 basis points, or half a percent) and if Greenspan announces a rate increase of 50bp, there should be no change in stock prices, since the stocks would already have been priced according to this expectation.

On the other hand, if rates rise higher than expected, stock prices must change to reflect the new reality and the overall market indices could be expected to fall. (Although, for example, stocks of financial corporations such as banks and other lenders may rise if a significant part of their revenues come from interest payments.)

34. Why is a firm's credit rating important?

The credit ratings are assigned by the major ratings agencies (Moody's, S&P, Fitch). Firms can raise cash by going to the equity markets (IPO, secondary offering, etc.) or through the debt markets (commercial paper, bonds, etc.). The credit rating directly affects the firm's cost of debt. The lower the rating, the higher the borrowing cost. If the rating is low enough, the firm may be rated non-investment grade, at which point many institutional investors will be prohibited from owning it. There are times when a firm will not be actively engaged in the capital markets. If a firm is rated AA, for example, it can pretty much raise cash whenever it wants by borrowing.

35. Why would a firm choose short-term over long-term debt?

Short-term debt is generally cheaper and easier to obtain, but risky because the lender can cut you off at any time, for example, if your credit rating worsens. If you borrow at a floating rate, the risk of short-term debt increases because of having to rollover — the short rate is now a random variable influenced by uncontrollable factors such as inflation. Short-term debt is appropriate only for short time horizons or when assets are liquid.

36. If a firm needs to raise cash by issuing a bond, but is worried about the fact that interest rates may drop in the future, what strategy should it employ?

It can issue long-term callable debt if it is concerned about locking in a high interest rate.

37. What is a leveraged buyout (LBO)? Why lever-up?

A leveraged buyout is a strategy to buy a company using borrowed funds. The acquiring company can use its own assets as collateral in anticipation that future cash flows from the resulting acquisition will cover the interest payments. LBOs enable shareholders to change the capital structure of the firm. They can buy up all of the stock and retire most of it, leaving the corporation with a structure, for example, of 90 percent debt and 10 percent equity. Benefits may include improved corporate governance: since debt payments have to be made, there are managerial incentives for good performance, thus better aligning managerial and shareholder interest.

38. How would you value a company with no earnings, such as a start-up?

You can't use the DDM or DCF. You would use multiples such as Price/Sales or comparables. Recall caveats in using comparables: in using comparables analysis, the key is to choose the right comparables. No two companies are exactly alike. Certainly it is necessary to choose companies in the same industry, but also consider the capital structure, size, operating margins and any seasonality effects.

39. Your boss uses the discounted free cash flow model to value high-growth stocks with low earnings. What do you think of this strategy?

It is very dangerous to value high-growth, low-earnings companies by the traditional DCF model. First of all, the distributions of important financial variables such as profit margins, working capital requirements, revenue growth rates, etc., are not distributed as they might be for more stable companies, but rather are bimodally distributed. The return on such a company is usually much better or much worse than expected, so traditional methods that trade off expected return with expected risk do not work.

Risk is very high, making it very difficult to determine an appropriate discount rate. This is the same problem faced by venture capitalists, who instead might just use a very high hurdle rate (the minimum return that someone must receive before they'll invest in something) of, say, 50% or so. Also, it is very difficult to determine the length of time over which the growth will occur, then diminish to stable growth. The uncertainty in all of these critical variables means that DCF analysis can produce very misleading and inaccurate results.

40. Why might high-tech stocks have high prices even though they have little or no earnings?

Investors are expecting high future growth.

41. How do you calculate a discount rate?

You would use the CAPM. While beta is an admittedly flawed estimate of risk, it is the best risk measure we have. The Capital Asset Pricing Model says that the proper discount rate to use is the risk-free rate plus the company risk premium, which reflects the particular company's market risk or beta.

42. What is beta?

Beta is a scalar measure of risk relative to the overall market. A financial instrument with a beta of 1 is perceived to be as risky as the market, and moves with the market. Note: Betas (βs) are always the weighted average of market values, not book values.

43. How do you calculate an equity beta?

You can perform a linear regression of the historical stock returns against market returns. The slope of the regression line is beta. Value Line, S&P and so on are data providers of equity beta. If you can't get beta (for example, if the company is private), use the beta of a comparable company as an estimate.

44. Is beta constant or does it vary over time?

As companies mature, beta should approach one in the limit. Some models of beta (for example, Barra) use a weighted average beta, giving 2/3 weight to the regression beta and weighting the rest at 1 to take this into account.

Thus $\beta = \frac{2}{3}\beta_{hist} + \frac{1}{3}$ (1)

45. What do you think the beta of General Motors is? What about a high-tech stock, such as Cisco Systems?

Since beta measures the sensitivity of the stock to the overall market, mature companies such as GM are generally expected to have betas close to 1. This means that they are about as risky as the overall market. A high-tech stock is perceived as more risky than the market and would probably have a beta higher than 1, perhaps closer to 2. Note that the more pronounced the growth orientation of the firm/industry, the higher beta is likely to be. Betas vary significantly between industries.

46. Why do you unlever beta?

You need a discount rate for free cash flows, which can be obtained through the CAPM: $E[r_{firm}] = E[r_{f}] + \beta_{firm}(r_{m} - r_{f})$. The beta of a firm is supposed to be an unbiased measure of the firm's risk. The firm value should be independent of the amount of financial leverage so you unlever out any miscellaneous debt. Since beta is a mathematical average of where the risk of the firm is concentrated among the creditors and shareholders, if the firm looks risky, is it risky because of the nature of the business or the nature of the financing? If the latter, you unlever beta to get at the business risk.

47. What is the weighted average cost of capital and how do you calculate it? Why is it important?

The weighted average cost of capital, WACC, is the expected return on a portfolio consisting of all of the entity's securities. It is used as the discount factor in capital budgeting decisions, and reflects the risk of the company. $WACC = r_A = r_E \, E/V + r_D \, D/V$ where r_E is the expected return on equity (return on stock), r_D is the cost of debt, E and D are the market values of equity and debt, respectively, and V is the market value of the firm, $V = D + E$. The WACC is used as the discount rate in valuation.

48. How would you calculate WACC for a private company?

If the company is not publicly traded, you would try to find comparable companies but include a control premium.

49. Why would a firm try to optimize its capital structure?

The idea here, due to MM (Modigliani-Miller), is that there is an optimal capital structure for a firm. The capital structure is the mix between debt and equity. If the capital structure is optimized, the return on equity (ROE) should also be optimized, because the firm possesses the optimal amount of equity to produce its income.

According to MM, firms should rely almost exclusively on debt to finance their operations. They don't do this, in practice, for a variety of reasons, including reduced liquidity, increased risk of financial distress, agency costs, etc.

50. What are some functions of an investment banker?

• Helps provide financing for a company by bringing new issues public. This involves performing due diligence and valuation analysis in order to price the issue.

- Acts as an intermediary between the investing public and security issuers.

- Provides advice and guidance to security issuers through and subsequent to offerings.

- May provide temporary stabilization of bid price during offering and distribution period.

51. How can a firm raise cash?

It can go to the capital markets (selling stock through an IPO or secondary offering), it can issue debt, or it can sell off assets.

Be prepared. Be very, very prepared.

Make sure you're prepared for your finance interviews with Vault's Career Guides and Career Services at the Vault Finance Career Channel. Go to http://finance.vault.com.

- For sample questions and overviews of important finance concepts, get the *Vault Guide to the Finance Interview* and the *Vault Guide to Advanced and Quantitative Finance Interviews*.

- For insider information about top employers, get the *Vault Guide to the Top 50 Finance Employers*, and Vault's Finance Employer Profiles, our 50-page reports on top firms, including Goldman Sachs, Morgan Stanley, Merrill, CSFB, J.P. Morgan Chase, Salomon Smith Barney, UBS Warburg and many more.

- For expert advice on specific careers, get the *Vault Career Guide to Investment Banking*, the *Vault Career Guide to Investment Management*, the *Vault Career Guide to Venture Capital*, and other Vault industry career guides.

- For one-on-one coaching with a finance interview expert, get Vault's Finance Interview Prep.

Increase your T/NJ Ratio
(Time to New Job)

Use the Internet's most targeted job search tools for finance professionals.

Vault Finance Job Board

The most comprehensive and convenient job board for finance professionals. Target your search by area of finance, function, and experience level, and find the job openings that you want. No surfing required.

VaultMatch Resume Database

Vault takes match-making to the next level: post your resume and customize your search by area of finance, experience and more. We'll match job listings with your interests and criteria and e-mail them directly to your inbox.

VAULT
> the insider career network™

SALES & TRADING

Skills for Sales & Trading

One thing an applicant for a sales and trading position should understand is that there are particular traits the interviewer wants. To begin with, most sales and trading professionals, from assistants and financial analysts all the way up to managing directors, sit on the same desk for virtually the entire workday. There are no offices or cubicles on a typical trading floor, which means that a salesperson or trader is quickly going to ask him or herself, "Is this someone I can work next to every day for the next few years?" As such, those with outgoing and friendly personalities tend to do better than those who come across as shy or abrasive. In addition, there are other skills sought by interviewers for these sorts of positions. In particular, for sales positions, the interviewer will wonder to him or herself: Does this person have good interpersonal skills?

In other words, will you be able to:

- Persuade and influence decision-making?
- Tactfully deal with demanding clients and co-workers?
- Advise clients and other constituents on investment decisions?
- Manage and expand your client base to increase profitability?
- Work efficiently under pressure?
- Handle effectively multiple tasks at one time?

They will also wonder: Do you have strong financial skills? Will you be able to:

- Understand how financial markets operate from a broad perspective as well as relative to a particular marketplace (i.e. the foreign exchange, stock, or treasury markets)?
- Communicate important quantitative investment criteria to a client base?

Do you have strong analytical skills? Will you be able to:

- Listen to the firm's analysts and strategists and also read and quickly interpret their research reports? Can you quickly and briefly relay the key ideas to clients?
- Evaluate the firm's competition and effectively market the firm against competition?

For trading positions, the interviewer will also want to know if you have good interpersonal skills as well as the following:

- Are you able to work efficiently under pressure?

- Can you handle and prioritize multiple tasks at one time? Can you do the same repeatedly throughout the day?

- Are you decisive?

- Can you manage people efficiently?

- Can you act as liaison between multiple (sometimes aggravated) parties?

Traders must also have good financial and analytical skills:

- Do you understand how financial markets operate from a broad perspective as well as relative to a particular marketplace (i.e. the foreign exchange, stock or treasury markets)?

- Will you be able to assess and/or initiate risk positions for various markets?

- Will you understand various products on a macro and micro level?

- Can you analyze and improve information flow among traders, clients, and salespeople on various on desks?

With these skills in mind, let us dive into some typical questions and effective answers for those of you seeking positions in sales and trading. These questions are not grouped together by topic, since a typical applicant will be asked completely unrelated questions throughout his or her interview process and is expected to able to shift gears quickly and continually (like an actual trader or salesperson).

Sales & Trading Questions

1. Why have you chosen sales and trading?

This is a rather basic question that often begins an interview, but it is one that could easily kill your chances before you really begin. You should give your own genuine answer to this drawing on your own skills and background. Even so, ou want to demonstrate that you are drawn to the activities and have the skills of a salesperson or trader. In other words, you like dealing with lots of people on the phone, you like a fast-paced environment, you work well under pressure, you like the entrepreneurial atmosphere of the trading floor, you like working on a team, you are interested in the markets. (Don't lie or be too specific about this last one, unless you are prepared to answer very specific follow-up questions.)

2. How do derivatives work?

Derivatives are financial instruments that derive their value from other more fundamental variables, such as the price movements stocks, bonds or commodities, interest rates changes, and even the prices of other derivatives. The most common classes of derivative securities are futures, forwards, swaps and options. Futures and forwards are contracts whereby two parties (say a large group of farmers and Unilever or Kellogg's) agree to a future trade at a specific time and price. Common types of futures include oil, cattle and U.S. Treasury bond futures. The main difference between forwards and futures is that futures trade in the open market (like stocks or bonds) whereas forwards are private contracts.

Swaps are similar to futures and forwards, but the agreements are for multiple trades in the future. For example, an insurance company might agree to pay the interest on a floating rate security it owns to a hedge fund that agrees to pay a fixed rate in return. This sort of agreement would be struck because the cash flows better match the two parties' risk profile and funding needs.

Options are contracts where two parties agree to a possible trade in the future ("possible" because one party has the right but not the obligation to complete the trade). If the buyer has the right, this is a "call." If the seller has the right, it is a "put."

Derivatives are used for three main purposes. Despite attention-grabbing headlines that suggest they are always exotic, volatile, and potentially very lucrative financial instruments, they are mainly used to hedge or provide financial insurance. Arbitrageurs also use them, seeking to exploit differences in prices for identical instruments in different markets in an attempt to earn a riskless profit. Finally, speculators looking to make spectacular profits use derivatives (which has led to news stories detailing the spectacular losses suffered by Barings, Orange County in California, and elsewhere). In a corporate finance role, you will mainly have to construct, pitch and/or evaluate simple as well as extremely complex derivative instruments for hedging and financial insurance.

3. What particular markets or instruments are you interested in?

You should be honest in answering this since it may lead to follow up questions on whatever market(s) you name. Remember, firms with rotational programs for entry-level analysts and associates (Citigroup, Bear, Lehman) want to hear that you are open to many different areas. This is true even if you have experience in a particular area. For lateral hires, they assume you will want to stay in the same sort of area.

4. Why debt, equity, or currency and commodities? Why cash or derivates?

Again, this should be answered honestly. Debt (or fixed income as it is often called) is viewed as more quantitative than equity. The debt markets are also more attuned to broad macroeconomic trends, such as interest rate changes and GDP figures. Equity is viewed as more "story telling" and as more microeconomic in nature. Derivatives are viewed as very quantitative and many would say that one can make money in derivatives whether or not the markets go up or down. One should be careful when answering this, however. Equity interviewers do not want to hear that you are NOT quantitative, and convertible bond desks are generally part of a firm's equity division but require knowledge of equities, bonds AND derivatives. Similarly, there is an element of "story telling" to areas of fixed income, particularly in high yield and emerging markets sales.

5. What previous experiences have you had that relate to sales and trading?

Hopefully you can demonstrate that your past experience relates to this skills listed at the beginning of this chapter. Any sort of sales or financial markets experience is relevant. Even if you have not sold or worked anywhere near "the Street," talk about your personal experience managing your E*TRADE account, or talk about the fast-paced and high-pressure environment of a past job, or about how you have been good at persuading people in the past.

6. Do you want to sell or trade?

Answer this honestly (you don't want to end up somewhere you will later regret). Again, firms with rotational programs want to know that you are open to movement.

7. What makes you think you can sell?

You should be able to demonstrate that you have the skills mentioned at the beginning of this chapter. If you have not sold for a living before, discuss ways in which you have persuaded people in the past.

8. How do you price an option?

While this question is typically asked in sales and trading interviews, it may also come up in a banking interview to test your basic financial knowledge. It may also come up at firms where derivative or convertible bond capital markets/origination is part of a banking rotation program. In addition, so-called "Real Options" are increasingly used in equity valuation, particularly in valuing pharmaceutical/biotech and natural resources-dependent companies.

There are two main ways to price an option. One is using a binomial pricing model. Binomial option pricing (which is also referred to as the two-state option-pricing model) is based on the theory that no arbitrage opportunities will become available, or if they do, they will be immediately arbitraged away. First introduced in 1979, binomial pricing and its variants are probably the most common model used for equity calls and puts today.

The binomial option pricing model is essentially based on the idea that an asset price will move up or down in a given time period in only one of two possible ways. For example, let us take a simple, two-step binomial model, where the initial price of a stock is 100. The price can either go up in the next time period to 110 or down to 90. The current risk-free (or U.S. Treasury) rate interest rate is 2%. How would we price a put with a strike price of 95? (That is, the right to sell the stock to the writer of the put at 95.)

$S = 100$, $u = 1.10$, $d = 0.90$, $K = 95$, and $r = 1.02$. The binomial "tree" thus looks like the following:

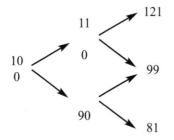

Thus the option payoffs (or what the payoffs would be if the put is not exercised until maturity) are:

Putuu= max $\{0, K-u^2S\} = 0$

Putud= max $\{0, K-udS\} = 0$

Putdu= max $\{0, K-duS\} = 0$

Putdd= max $\{0, K-d^2S\} = 14$

In other words, only if the put goes down twice is it "in the money" or below the $95 strike price. Otherwise, it is worthless.

Since $r=1.02$, the risk neutral probability p is:

P= $(r-d)/(u-d)$ or $(1.02-0.90)/(1.10-0.90) = 0.60$

If we look at step dS=90, the value from immediate exercise of the option is (K-dS) or 5; at uS = 110, (K-uS) = -115. The value from not exercising would be 0 if the price of the stock goes up or $Put_{dd}= 14$ if the price goes down again. Using the risk-neutral probability and discounting by the risk-free rate, the value from not exercising here is:

$(1/1.02)[(0.60)(0) + (0.40)(14)] = 5.49$

Immediate exercise at the first step of S=100 leads to a payoff of $\max\{K-S,0\} = -5$; since it is not optimal to exercise with a negative result, it is effectively $\max\{K-S,0\} = 0$. Not exercising leads to $Put_u = 0$ if step uS is the result, and $Put_d = 5.49$ if dS is the result. Since (again) it is not optimal to exercise early at the first step, the initial value of the put is:

$P = (1/1.02)[(0.60)(0)+(0.40)(5.49)] = 2.15$

Now imagine taking this process out hundreds or even thousands of steps. You can see why you will not be asked to solve a problem like this in an interview. As an options salesperson or trader, complex computer programs thankfully cacluclate binomial pricing.

The other way to price options is by using the Black-Scholes equation, which was first proposed in 1973. The original version of the equation assumed that all options were "European" (which means that they cannot be exercised before maturity) and do not pay dividends.

A call option can be valued by the Black-Scholes equation using these variables:

S = Current price of the underlying asset (stock or otherwise)

K = Strike price of the option (sometimes called "X" for exercise price instead)

t = Time until the option expires

r = Riskless interest rate (should be for time period closest to lifespan of option)

σ^2 = Variance in the log-normal value of the underlying asset (volatility)

Once one has these variables, one plugs them into this equation:

Price of call $= SN(d_1) - Ke^{-rt}N(d_2)$

Price of put $= Ke^{-rt}N(-d_2) - SN(-d_1)$

When

$$d_1 = \frac{\ln(S/K)+(r + \sigma^2/2)t}{\sigma \sqrt{t}}$$

and

$$d_2 = d_1 - \sigma\sqrt{t}$$

Dividend payments reduce the price of a stock (you may have noticed that a stock's price almost always declines on the ex-dividend day). The equation was later modified to take steady dividend payments into account. If the dividends payable on the underlying asset are expected to remain constant over the life of the option, the equation becomes.

$$C \text{ (call)} = Se^{-yt}N(d_1) - Ke\text{-}rtN(d_2)$$

$$P \text{ (put)} = Ke^{-rt}[1\text{-}N(d_2)] - Se^{-yt}[1\text{-}N(d_1)]$$

When

y (yield) = annual dividend/price of the asset

and

$$d_1 = \frac{\ln(S/K) + (r-y+\sigma^2/2)t}{\sigma\sqrt{t}}$$

and

$$d_2 = d_1 - \sigma\sqrt{t}$$

"N(d)" is the probability that such a variable will be less than "d" on a standard normal distribution. These values can be found (or approximated) using a computer.

As already stated, you will never actually have to price an option during an interview, but it is important that you be able to tell your interviewer the two main pricing methods (Binomial and Black-Scholes) and the basic elements that go into determining price under both methods: current price of the underlying asset, strike price of the option, time until option expiration, risk-free interest rate, volatility in price of the underlying asset, and dividends (if applicable).

9. Tell me what an institutional investor is.

Buyers of stocks, bonds, and other investment instruments are generally governments, corporations, individual investors (either "retail" like people buying through Schwab or Merrill Lynch or via a trust or private bank like J.P. Morgan for the very wealthy) and institutional investors. Institutional investors are non-governmental institutions that manage and invest money for themselves or others. They include mutual funds, which pool and manage money for large groups of retail investors; pension funds, which handle retirement money for a company's or state's defined benefit retirement plan; insurance companies, which invest either to earn enough to pay out policies in the future or to hedge their liabilities; and endowment funds (like a museum's left-over donation money or a university endowment). Certain professional investment firms (like Fidelity or the Capital Group) manage money on an outsourced basis for both retail clients through mutual funds as well as for institutions like endowments or for government or corporate clients. These are also commonly referred to as institutional investors. Hedge funds are often lumped in with institutional investors. Some firms break sales coverage (especially in derivatives) into "corporate" (non-pension-related), "insurance", "hedge funds" and "institutional" (everything else save individual investors).

10. Does the price of an option go up or down when interest rates rise?

This is a classic trick question in two ways. First, most interviewees have drilled it into their heads that when interest rates go up, bond prices go down and vice versa. Thus, your gut reaction is to say "down." Don't rush to answer this one — the question is about options, not bonds. Second, the answer depends on what kind of options one is talking about. If it is a call, the price will go up when interest rates rise. If it is a put, the price will decrease. One can explain this several ways. If you are very comfortable with math and the Black-Scholes equation, you might see that as "r" goes up, "C" does as well, while "P" decreases.

$$C \text{ (call)} = Se^{-yt}N(d_1) - Ke^{-rt}N(d_2)$$

$$P \text{ (put)} = Ke^{-rt}[1-N(d_2)] - Se^{-yt}[1-N(d_1)]$$

When

y (yield) = annual dividend/price of the asset

and

$$d_1 = \frac{\ln(S/K) + (r-y+\sigma^2/2)t}{\sigma\sqrt{t}}$$

and

$$d_2 = d_1 - \sigma\sqrt{t}$$

Basically, money now is worth more than money later, and as interest rates rise, the net present value of the final exercise price is reduced. According to the Black-Scholes equation, we price options as though we are in a risk-neutral economy, which means that we assume that the underlying security's price will bring future returns equal to the risk-free interest rate. Let us take a world with two periods, 1 (today) and 2 (tomorrow). If the call option is ever in the money in the future, it will pay us S_2-K. The present value of this payment is $(S_2$-K)/(1+r)$, or $(S_2/1)+K/(1+r)$. Since the underlying security appreciates by 1+r, $S_2=(S_1)(1+r)$, the present value of a possible future payoff is $S_1 (1+r)/[(1+r)-(K/1+r)]$.

For puts, the put valuation equation breaks down into: put = call + the present value of the strike price - the underlying stock price + the present value of dividends. A put is the right to sell something at a set price at a future date. Rising interest rates makes the present value of what you will get less valuable, all else being equal. Alternatively, just think of what one would have to do if one could not invest in options but wanted the same result: one would sell short an amount of the stock (represented by Δ) and lend out the present value of the strike price weighted by the probability of paying the strike price at expiration. (In options parlance, Δ, or "delta," is the amount of the underlying needed to produce the replicating portfolio.)

Since owning a bond is equivalent to lending, and the price of a bond goes down when interest rates rise, the value of a put will similarly fall when interest rates rise. Of course, when interest rates rise or fall, the overall stock market often moves in the opposite direction, which is why we state "all else being equal." In the real world, changes in interest rates might affect the underlying price enough to offset the predicted change in an option's price using Black-Scholes. (For example, interest rates rising should increase the value of a call but the underlying stock of an interest-rate sensitive company like a commercial bank may go down as a result of the rate increase.)

The way in which the various option valuation inputs affect value is summarized in the chart on the next page.

CHANGE IN INPUTS AND AFFECT ON OPTION VALUATION		
INPUT CHANGE	CALL VALUE	PUT VALUE
UNDERLYING ASSET'S PRICE GOES UP	GOES UP	GOES DOWN
OPTION STRIKE PRICE GOES UP	GOES DOWN	GOES UP
VOLATILITY IN PRICE OF UNDERLYING ASSET GOES UP	GOES UP	GOES UP
TIME TO EXPIRATION INCREASES	GOES UP	GOES UP
INTEREST RATES GOES UP	GOES UP	GOES DOWN
INCREASE IN DIVIDENDS PAID	GOES DOWN	GOES UP

11. What would happen to the price of an option if Iraq invaded Kuwait again?

Increases in volatility are good for option prices, all else being equal, because the more prices jump around, the more likely an option will expire "in the money." Thus, an invasion, in theory, would increase the value of all options. In practice, the overall stock market might plunge, while certain sectors would soar (such as defense and energy). Therefore it is unlikely that all else would remain equal. It is likely that underlying prices would fall enough in certain sectors (like airlines or brokerage stocks) to cancel out whatever gains were created by a spike in volatility. Thus, there is no unambiguous answer to this question.

12. What are some limitations of the Black-Scholes equation?

The Black-Scholes equation applies only to European-style options. American-style options are generally more valuable (all else being equal) than European options since the holder of an American option can exercise the option at any time before maturity (European option holders can only exercise at maturity). In addition, the Black-Scholes formula assumes that asset price changes follow a lognormal distribution. In reality, though, prices can jump around far more than what a normal distribution would predict, and thus the actual distribution can have fatter tails than a normal distribution. This means that there is a greater chance of an option being exercised than suggested by the formula. Thus, option prices (European- and American-style) tend to be slightly higher in real world.

13. What do you do for fun?

This is a fairly common question for sales and trading interviews. You should try to think of something truthful yet interesting that will help you stand out. Remember, salespeople and traders tend to be outgoing and gregarious types, so athletics, outdoor activities, or something totally unique like being in a band would go over better than, say, macramé.

14. What is a yield curve and how is it constructed?

A yield curve is the plot of current spot yields against maturity. For example, a Bloomberg machine (a good comment to make if you are interviewing with a data vendor – know their product and refer to it in your answers) continually updates the current yield curve.

The yield curve is constructed of current, on-the-run benchmark Treasuries. An example yield curve is shown below.

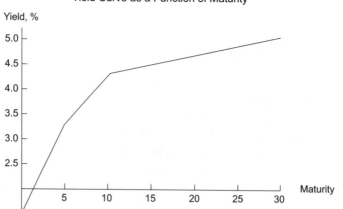

Yield Curve as a Function of Maturity

As noted previously, the shape of the yield curve can be upward sloping (normal), downward sloping (or inverted), flat, humped and so on. "Missing" maturities such as one-year, three-year and so on may be obtained by straight linear interpolation. In order for this method to be valid, we assume that the yield curve is constructed of piecewise linear segments. The missing one-year value, then, would be estimated by interpolating between the closest given points that bound it. In this case, we have the six-month yield and the two-year yield and nothing in between. The general interpolation formula is derived from the first order Taylor series approximation of f, where f is the continuous function of yields:

$$f(x) = x_0 + f'(x_0)(x - x_0)$$

Now, we estimate the derivative as $f'(x0) = \dfrac{\Delta y}{\Delta x} = \dfrac{y}{x}$

Here, y_1, y_0, x_1 and x_0 are known, and x is the point about which we seek the estimate. Here, x = 1 year, x_0 = 0.5 years, x_1 = 2 years, y_0 = yield at 0.5 years = 1.61% and y_1 = yield at 2 years = 2.13%. Then, f(1) = f(0.5) + (2.13-1.61)/(2-0.5)(1- 0.5) = 1.61% + [(2.13-1.61)/(2-0.5)](1- 0.5) = 1.78%.

There are par yield curves, forward yield curves and spot yield curves. If the yield curve is upward sloping, the forward yield curve is above the spot curve, which is above the par yield curve. If the yield curve is downward sloping, the par yield curve is above the spot curve which is above the forward curve.

Some definitions:

- **On-the-run:** Newly auctioned securities are referred to as "on-the-run" while older, seasoned issues (i.e., those sold in previous auctions) are referred to as "off-the-run."

- **Benchmark Treasury:** A benchmark Treasury is a reference Treasury having a specific maturity, such as three months, two years and so on. These are securities against which other bonds may be measured, usually in terms of yield comparison. The news media will often say things like, "The benchmark 10-year Treasury closed up 30 basis points."

- **Basis point:** A basis point is 1/100th of a percentage point. If someone says that the yield on the two-year benchmark treasury rose by 100bp, they mean that the yield increased by 100 (1/100th) percentage points, or a full one percent. Basis points provide us with a convenient means to speak of fractions of percentage points. They can be used to report the cost of borrowing in terms of a spread to some reference, as in, "Ford Credit issued bonds at 25 bp over LIBOR," implying that the cost of borrowing was LIBOR + 0.25% — that is, if LIBOR is 4%, the total borrowing cost would be 4.25%.

15. Define the term structure of interest rates.

The term structure of interest rates is the relationship between yield to maturity of risk-free zero coupon securities (usually Treasuries) and their maturities. The yield of a newly issued risk-free zero coupon bond (pure discount bond) is called the spot rate, and the relationship between these spot rates and the bond maturities is called the spot yield curve.

16. What is a spot rate?

The spot rate is the rate at which you could purchase the asset today. There are spot interest rates, spot rates for currencies, spot prices for commodities and so forth.

17. What is a forward rate?

A forward rate is an interest rate prevailing at some later time that can be locked in today. For example, if we are going to need a one-year loan in one year's time, we could go to the bank today and lock in the rate we will pay. We can get an idea of the market's opinion of where forward rates will be by calculating them from the yield curve.

18. Do forward rates predict the rates that ultimately prevail in later periods?

No. The expectation is that forward rates are unbiased predictors of future spot rates, but in practice, numerous studies (most notably one by Fama in 1976 and another paper by Fama in 1984) have shown that forward rates have very low predictive power over long time periods. Fama found mixed results over different time intervals: for example, he found one-month forward rates have some predictive power to forecast the spot rate one month ahead. Since the forward rate embeds two elements – the expected future spot rate and the risk premium – he hypothesized that this is due to the failure of models to control for this term premium in the forward rates. Unless this risk premium is controlled for, the best use of forward rates may just be as insight into the market's opinion of future spot rates.

19. I was just looking at Bloomberg and noticed that I can earn 3.872% on a one-year bond in the U.K. and can borrow at 2% here in the U.S. Can I make a risk-free profit by doing this?

Not necessarily. The reason for different interest rates across countries is primarily due to different expectations of inflation. High interest rates in the U.K. relative to the U.S. indicate that the currency is expected to depreciate relative to the U.S. dollar.

20. If you were trading for a pension fund, would you recommend tax-free munis or corporate bonds? Why?

Corporates. The pension fund is already tax-exempt so it would be disadvantageous to invest in tax-free munis, which offer lower rates than corporates due to the tax-free status.

21. Why are yields on corporate bonds higher than treasury bonds of the same maturity?

Because of the risk involved. Treasury bonds are generally considered to be risk-free, "backed by the full faith and credit of the United States Government." Corporate bonds will involve some risk of default, credit downgrades and so on, so investors demand a higher yield (lower price) in order to compensate them for the increased risk of the corporate bond.

22. Does treasury stock receive dividends? Is it included in market capitalization of a company? What happens to a company's ROE if shares are repurchased?

Treasury stock does not receive dividends. It is not included in market capitalization of a company, since market cap includes only outstanding shares. Retirement of stock through corporate repurchases raises financial variables such as ROE and EPS since the number of outstanding shares, used in the denominator of these variables, decreases.

23. What is LIBOR? Why is it important?

The London InterBank Offered Rate. It is important because LIBOR is the primary reference rate used in the Euromarkets. Even in the U.S., many floating rates are quoted as LIBOR plus or minus a spread. For example, in a swap the floating payer may be quoted as paying LIBOR + 25bp.

24. What is a defensive stock?

Defensive stock is the stock of a company that is not affected much by downturns in the economy. It may be used as a diversification element in a client portfolio. Defensive stocks typically include stocks of corporations that manufacture consumer essentials, such as food, clothing, pharmaceuticals, and so on, which people would still need even during recessions. On the other hand, stocks in sectors such as automotive, heavy construction or steel are highly sensitive to economic conditions.

25. A U.S. Government bond is selling in the market at 96.25. What is the price of this bond?

Prices are quoted as a percentage of par in "32nds", so "96.25" means 96 and 25/32%. 25/32 is close to 24/32 = 6/8 = ¾ so the price is about 96.78% of par, say "96.75% per $1,000 face" or $967.5 per $1,000 face. This is a discount bond, meaning it sells below par.

26. A prisoner was to be executed but, after begging for his life, was given one chance to live. He was given 100 balls, 50 black and 50 white, and told to distribute them evenly between two urns in any way he liked. He would then draw a ball at random from one of the urns, and his life would be spared if the ball were white. Legend has it that he drew a white ball and was released. What possible strategy could he have used to maximize his chances of success?

If he had just distributed the balls evenly among the two urns, then his chances would have been 50-50 no matter which urn he drew. So he put one white ball in urn A and the other 49 white balls in urn B, along with the remaining 50 black balls. If he was handed urn A, he had a certainty of drawing a white ball, and if handed urn B, he had only a slightly less than 50-50 (49/99, to be exact)chance of drawing a white ball. His total probability of drawing a white ball was therefore ½ x 1 + ½ x 49/99 = 74/99, just slightly less than 75%.

27. If you believe that there is a 40% chance of earning a 10% return on a stock, a 50% change of losing 5% and a 10% chance of losing 20%, what is the expected gain/(loss) on the stock?

The expected return is the weighted average of the probabilities of the returns times the returns, or

$$E[R] = \sum_{i=1}^{n} w_i E[R] \text{ so } E[R] = 0.40(+10\%) + 0.50(-5\%) + 0.1(-20\%) = -0.5\%.$$

Be prepared. Be very, very prepared.

Make sure you're prepared for your finance interviews with Vault's
Career Guides and Career Services at the Vault Finance Career Channel.
Go to http://finance.vault.com.

- For sample questions and overviews of important finance concepts, get
  the *Vault Guide to the Finance Interview* and the *Vault Guide to
  Advanced and Quantitative Finance Interviews*.

- For insider information about top employers, get the *Vault Guide to the
  Top 50 Finance Employers*, and Vault's Finance Employer Profiles, our
  50-page reports on top firms, including Goldman Sachs, Morgan
  Stanley, Merrill, CSFB, J.P. Morgan Chase, Salomon Smith Barney,
  UBS Warburg and many more.

- For expert advice on specific careers, get the *Vault Career Guide to
  Investment Banking*, the *Vault Career Guide to Investment
  Management*, the *Vault Career Guide to Venture Capital*, and other
  Vault industry career guides.

- For one-on-one coaching with a finance interview expert, get Vault's
  Finance Interview Prep.

RESEARCH/
INVESTMENT
MANAGEMENT

Skills for Research and Investment Management

Not all research analyst positions are the same. To begin with, analysts generally work on the "Sell" or the "Buy" side, meaning they work either for investment banks/brokerage firms that sell securities, or for mutual funds, insurance companies, hedge funds and others that buy securities. At sell-side firms, the analysts who cover stocks may get the most press coverage, but all of the larger firms also have analysts who cover various types of bonds and hybrid securities. Additionally, they have investment strategists and economists, who can be considered analysts.

Several firms also have "specialty" equity salespeople, who are a cross between institutional salespeople and analysts and who focus on broad sectors such as healthcare or technology. On the buy side, there are analysts and/or portfolio managers who buy stocks, bonds, derivative products, and even real estate. While certain traits are shared by those on the buy and sell side, and while many analysts spend time on both sides of the divide during their careers, we have separated the desired skills into two sections.

Buy-side skills

Your exact duties will vary depending on where you are applying. Nonetheless, your interviewer will most likely be trying to determine:

- Will you be able to analyze and quickly understand single company information, industry-wide issues, and macro-economic trends?

- Are you good at building ongoing relationships with, and getting information from sell-side analysts and salespeople, company management, suppliers, industry experts and others from whom you will gain data?

- Do you understand various valuation methods (discounted cash flow techniques, comparable company analysis, etc.)?

- Are you an expert at accounting (or economics, if applicable)?

- Will you be able to accurately project earnings, cash flow statements, balance sheets, and/or overall industry, market and economic trends?

- Can you effectively communicate investment ideas and recommendations to your firm's investment committee and the media? Can you defend those same ideas?

- If you become part of your firm's decision-making process, will you able to successfully evaluate investment recommendations?

- Are you personally passionate about the market?

- Are you able to understand risk levels of various investments and balance your firm's exposure to various sectors in order to keep risk levels tolerable?

- Are you assertive, autonomous, probing and innovative?

Sell-side skills

Whether covering stocks, bonds, the entire market or the economy as a whole, your interview will essentially be trying to find out:

- Will you be able to analyze and quickly understand single company information, industry-wide issues, and macro-economic trends?

- Are you good at building ongoing relationships with, and getting information from, company management, suppliers, industry experts and others from whom you will gain data?

- Are you assertive, autonomous, probing and innovative?

- Will you be able to get along with bankers, salespeople, and traders?

- Are you very good at financial modeling, especially when using Excel?

- Do you understand various valuation methods (discounted cash flow techniques, comparable analysis, etc.)?

- Are you an expert at accounting (or economics if applicable)?

- Will you be able to accurately project earnings, cash flow statements, balance sheets, and/or overall industry, market and economic trends?

- Can you effectively communicate investment ideas and recommendations to institutional clients, retail customers, the media, bankers, salespeople, traders, and bankers, in person, via email and on the phone? Can you defend those same ideas?

- Do you have good presentation and marketing skills?

- Will you be able to bring in new business to the firm (either new institutional investors or banking clients)?

- Can you produce well-written morning call notes, updates and research reports on companies, industries and/or economics under tight deadlines?

- Are you a stickler for detail and extremely well organized?

- Are you personally passionate about the market?

The following pages include some specific questions asked during past research interviews along with possible answers.

Research/Investment Management Questions

1. Why buy- vs. sell-side (or vice versa)?

There are several good responses to this question, and you should tailor your response so that it is truthful and fits in with your goals. If you are interviewing for both buy and sell side positions, you should be honest about this and talk about your interest in uncovering undervalued securities. You should also make certain that your answers mesh with the desired skills mentioned above.

If you are going for only buy- or sell-side positions, you should not deride the area you are not interested in. Many of your interviewers will have spent part of their career on both sides of the divide. You should also not state that you want the buy side because you think the hours are better (even though they generally are) because you don't want to come across as lazy.

You also don't want to say that you want the sell-side because you want to focus on a particular industry. Most brokerages only place new associates in particular areas if they have expertise (i.e. someone who worked at Disney before business school in the media group, or a medical doctor in health care). Financial analysts are even less likely to get the group they want. Most likely, you will end up wherever there is an opening. So even if you really want biotech, be prepared to cover the automobile industry. (Note: like in sales and trading and in banking, sell-side research hires just out of undergrad are generally called "financial analysts," "analysts" or "F.A.s." The next level is associate (usually those with MBAs and/or CFAs), while "research analysts" are generally those who are at the assistant vice president (AVP) level or above.)

2. What courses have you taken/will take to prepare you for a career in asset management/research?

Again, discuss any accounting, finance or economics courses you have taken or will take in the following year(s) if it is a summer position. Do not forget to discuss other less-obvious courses, like "Conflict Resolution" or the like, since they too can be relevant. If you have any professional designations (even pending) like a C.P.A., C.F.A., or M.D., certainly mention them.

3. What would you buy? What would you short?

This is a variation of the earlier stock pitch question. If you are interviewing for a position in fixed income, derivatives, or strategy research, you might want to have some idea what sort of bonds or derivatives analysts find attractive. For example, if you believe that there will be increased tension in the Middle East, you might argue that one should go long on volatility in the oil sector. If you expect inflation to pick up, you might suggest shorting inflation-sensitive bonds (since an increase in inflation generally leads to an increase in interest rates and thus a decrease in existing bond prices.)

4. What do you think about index funds? Do you subscribe to the "Random Walk" theory?

Those who tout index funds (funds that do not pick stocks but rather mimic a particular index like the S&P 500 or the Dow Jones Eurostoxx 50) and the author of *A Random Walk Down Wall Street* (Burton Gordon Malkiel) maintain that on average, most active portfolio managers and sell-side analysts underperform the broader stock market. Many studies have supported this theory (often called the "efficient markets theory"). Supporters of this view maintain that investors should not pay the extra fees that active mutual fund managers and stockbrokers charge, but should simply buy index funds.

You do believe in investors diversifying their holdings, but unless you are interviewing at Vanguard or another index fund/firm, you do NOT believe in what the author of *Random Walk* says or that investors should use index funds. You believe that a good stock (or bond) picker can find mispriced securities and/or exploit the market's occasional inefficiencies. Just think about it: if everyone believed in the efficient markets theory, no one would buy mutual funds, invest in hedge funds, or use the advice of sell-side analysts. Your interviewers would all be out of work. Do not fall into this trap during an interview, no matter what your finance professor told you in class.

> **5. Stocks historically outperform bonds over the long term. If I am a long-term investor, I don't need any bonds in my portfolio. True or false?**

This is false. It is true that measured both arithmetically and geometrically, stocks in the U.S. (as measured by the S&P or Dow Jones Industrial indexes) have outperformed the various key bond categories since at least 1926. However, when the broader stock market rises, bonds tend to go down, and vice versa, and there is not perfect covariance. You should be familiar with the phrase "No risk, no reward." Higher returning assets tend to be riskier than lower returning assets. By having a certain amount of bonds in a portfolio, one can exploit the lack of perfect covariance in order to earn the same return with lower risk. Let's take the simple example of a two-security portfolio to illustrate:

First, let's assume that these securities have a single period investment horizon, that returns are independent between periods, that there are no transactions costs, and that the assets' returns follow a normal distribution.

Next, let's say that $\mu p = X_1 \mu_1 + X_2 \mu_2 =$ the portfolio's expected return where $\mu =$ the mean return and where $X =$ the probability of occurrence so in this case, $X_1 + X_2 = 1$. Let's also state $R =$ return of the security or portfolio in question.

Further, the variance of the return on this two-security portfolio is represented by the term:

$\sigma^2 = X_1^2 \sigma_1^2 + X_2^2 \sigma_2^2 + 2 X_1 X_2$ Covariance (R_1, R_2). (Note: The variance (σ^2) and standard deviation (σ) of the portfolio are NOT a weighted average of the individual securities' σ^2 and σ since $X_1^2 + X_2^2 \neq 1$.) Finally, let's define ρ as

$$\rho = \frac{\text{Cov } (R_1, R_2)}{\sigma_1 \sigma_2}$$

when:

$r = +1$ there is perfect positive correlation,

$r = 0$ there is no correlation whatsoever, and

$r = -1$ perfect negative correlation

Thus:

$$\sigma^2 = X_1^2 \sigma_1^2 + X_2^2 \sigma_2^2 + 2 X_1 X_2 \rho \sigma_1 \sigma_2$$

Let's take a simple case where the securities can return 0 or 100:

	R₁	R₂	E[R]	δ²	POSSIBLE RESULTS
X1 = 1	0%	100%	50%	HIGH	100, 0
X2 = 1	0%	100%	50%	HIGH	100, 0
X1 = 0.5 X2 = 0.5	0%	100%	50%	LOWER	100, 0,50, 50

In this case, risk is lower even though the mean return is the same in all three cases. If $\rho < 1$, one will have the same expected return with diversification.

Graphically, the risk-reward trade-offs can be shown in the following three illustrations:

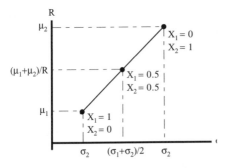

$\rho = +1$; There is perfect correlation between assets 1 and 2 and no gain or loss from diversification.

$$\sigma^2 = X_1^2 \sigma_1^2 + X_2^2 \sigma_2^2 + 2 X_1 X_2 \sigma_1 \sigma_2$$
$$\sigma^2 = (X_1 \sigma_1 + X_2 \sigma_2)^2$$
$$\sigma = X_1 \sigma_1 + X_2 \sigma_2$$

$\rho = -1$; There is perfect negative correlation. Here, at point "J", d is zero. One can achieve higher returns with less risk!

$$\sigma^2 = X_1^2 \sigma_1^2 + X_2^2 \sigma_2^2 - 2 X_1 X_2 \sigma_1 \sigma_2$$
$$\sigma^2 = (X_1 \sigma_1 - X_2 \sigma_2)^2$$
$$\sigma = X_1 \sigma_1 + X_2 \sigma_2$$
$$X_1 \sigma_1 - X_2 \sigma_2 = 0$$
$$X_1 = \delta 2/(\sigma_1 + \sigma_2)$$
$$\rho = 0$$

Generally, covariance is between 1 and 0, so the risk-reward line will be curved rather than angular. Still, as long as securities' returns are not perfectly correlated, one can construct a two-security portfolio with a higher return and less risk than one could earn with just one security.

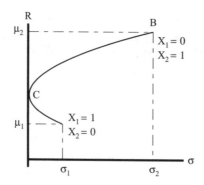

This notion can be expanded to include a portfolio with dozens, hundreds, or even thousands of securities. Therefore, in theory at least, if one can find the appropriate uncorrelated assets (of technology stocks and grocery store stocks, or of stocks in general and bonds, or of bonds and gold, etc.), a portfolio manager can use bonds to lower the risk in his or her portfolio without lowering returns.

6. How would you invest $1 million today?

You should be able to weave in specific recommendations for long or short pitches with an overall investment theme. You should know what you are talking about when you answer this — don't B.S.. Ask friends or alumni in the industry for their advice on this, read investment strategy research reports if you can, or at the very least investment advice articles in *BusinessWeek* if you are totally clueless. A typical answer might be something like: "I would invest $200,000 in these four specific stocks [give brief versions of your pitches if you have not already], $300,000 in U.S. small caps, since they tend to outperform large caps in the early stages of a recovery, $200,000 in East Asian equities, since the U.S recovery should lead to increased exports for the Asian economies, and $300,000 in a mixture of investment-grade and high-yield corporate bonds."

7. What investment philosophy do you subscribe to and why?

There are several main investment strategies:

- **"Aggressive growth"** investors want to maximize rapid capital appreciation. This implies a readiness for high risk. It may also imply the use of alternative investment vehicles like private equity, venture capital, derivatives and hedge funds.

- **"Growth"** investors seek capital appreciation, but with less risk than "aggressive growth investors." (And thus lower returns.) This still usually means stocks rather than bonds.

- **"Income"** investors concentrate on current and steady income. Such investors usually have a mix of bonds and preferred stocks. They may also have dividend paying stocks and coupon-bearing convertible bonds, usually from "blue chip" companies like IBM or G.E.

- **"Growth-income"** or **"balanced"** investors seek a mix of "Growth" and "Income."

- **"Conservative"** or **"defensive"** investors seek capital preservation at all cost. This means investing in only high-grade bonds and the like.

There are a few main investment styles, including:

- **"Value"** investing, which emphasizes securities (mainly stocks) that have a market price far below whatever value analysts have computed for the security, whether based on DCF, P/E, or what have you.

- **"Contrarian"** investing, which means investing contrary to the current market direction or beliefs. This is an exaggerated version of value investing, since contrarians seek out-of-favor investments with the potential for large gains through turnarounds.

- **"Momentum investors"** or **"market timers"** use economic figures or technical analysis to make investment decisions rather than fundamental analysis. The idea is to be invested when prices are rising, and sell just as the market begins falling. This style generally uses technical analysis to time an investment in a particular stock or bond. The goal is to invest at a time when the security's price movement can be anticipated.

Additional common terms:

- **"Fundamental analysis"** means using DCF, P/E, talking with management, examining the income statement and balance sheet or other "fundamental" techniques to value a security.

- **"Technical analysis"** means basing investment decisions by analyzing price charts, trading volume, "resistance levels," and the like. Technical analysts do not care about management, the balance sheet, earnings, or other fundamentals.

- **"Indexing"** or **"passive investing"** means not picking individual securities but rather mimicking a particular index like the S&P 500 or the Dow Jones Eurostoxx 50. Adherents maintain that, on average, most active portfolio managers and sell-side analysts under perform the broader market. Many studies have supported this theory (often called the "efficient markets theory").

There is no one correct answer to this question at a buy-side interview. You should make sure you know which styles and philosophies the firm employs before the interview and make sure your answer is in line with what the firm espouses. On the sell side, most analysts would consider themselves fundamental analysts, but are agnostic when it comes to growth versus income. Few believe in technical analysis (since it means that what they do is meaningless), though many sell-side firms have technical analysts, so be careful not to downplay any one technique, style or philosophy.

8. What would you do if a stock you just recommended lost 10% – 15% of its value?

Situations like this happen quite frequently on the buy and sell side alike. You should prepare an answer to a question like this one that demonstrates that you are level headed, analytical, articulate, and able to learn from any mistakes you may have made.

9. Are you a top-down or bottom-up investor?

Top-down investors evaluate the economy as a whole and find which sectors they believe will outperform the broader market and invest in these. For example, if the economy is entering a recession, such investors may seek "recession-proof" stocks like Kraft or Phillip Morris. If oil prices are expected to rise, they might seek energy sector investments. Bottom-up investors seek investments that are compelling values based on fundamental analysis (DCF, relative valuation or otherwise) regardless of overall economic conditions. Many portfolio managers are a combination of both. If you are interviewing at a buy-side firm, you should research the firm's philosophy and match your answer accordingly.

10. In 2002 the S&P is trading at a P/E multiple much higher than it was in the 1970s or even during the booming 1980s. Does this mean that stocks as a whole are currently overvalued?

It does not necessarily mean that they are overvalued. Mathematically, we can show that P/E can be broken down as follows:

Using the Dividend Discount Method of Valuation, P=DPS/(r-g). If we divide both sides by EPS, one gets:

P/E = Payout Ratio(1+g)/(r-g)

Using the FCFE method of valuation:

P = FCFE/(r-g), and

P/E = (FCFE/Earnings)(1+g)/(r-g)

All else being equal, higher growth means higher P/E ratios. All else being equal, lower interest rates mean lower discount rates and thus also higher P/E ratios. One could argue whether corporate earnings were growing faster than in the 1970s and 1980s. Interest rates in 2002 were clearly far lower, however, which allows all stocks to trade at higher multiples.

11. What kinds of things make a stock extremely volatile in the short term?

Uncertainty about the economy or the sector that a stock is in; varying news from competitors (for example, if Ford says business is weak but GM says it is strong, Daimler Chrysler's stock may move about wildly until it discusses its outlook); the firm may be in a highly cyclical sector (like semiconductors or oil); lots of momentum players in the stock (these are investors who bet that the direction of a stock will continue rather than those who perform fundamental analysis); the company may be in a newer, less proven and/or high growth industry (like biotech); and legislative uncertainty (will the government raise or lower tariffs for steel makers?).

12. How do you calculate the return on a stock?

The return on a stock is calculated as the percentage change in price over the investment horizon. If P_0 is the price at the beginning of the investment horizon and P1 is the price at the end of the horizon, then

$$r = \frac{P_1 + D - P_0}{P_0}$$

where D is the total of dividends paid over the period.

13. What is an option?

An option is a contract between buyer and seller that provides the buyer the right, but not the obligation, to enter into a transaction at some future date, while the seller is obliged to honor the transaction. Options are derivatives that depend on the value of the underlying. For instance, one can buy a call option on a specific stock. The option will be defined by the exercise price (strike price) and the time to expiry. As an example, you buy a June call option on IBM stock with a strike of $80 when IBM is trading at $75. This gives you the option to purchase IBM at a price equal to the strike price, before or at the expiration date depending on whether the option is European or American style.

14. What is put-call parity? How is it used?

Put-call parity provides a relationship between call and put prices on a stock that should hold in equilibrium. It is based on a no-arbitrage argument, and asserts that $p + S_0 = c + Xe^{-rT}$, where p and c are the price of the put and call, respectively, S_0 the stock price, X the strike price, r the risk-free rate, and T the time to expiry of the options. It is used to find the price of a put having strike X and time to expiry T, if the price of the call with the same parameters is known, and vice versa. It can also be used to determine whether arbitrage opportunities exist: given observed put and call prices, stock and exercise prices and time to expiry, one can use put-call parity to determine an implied interest rate. Comparing to the available rate will allow a decision to be made on whether the market prices permit an arbitrage opportunity.

15. Can you describe a situation when it would be optimal to exercise an American call option before the expiry date? Does it matter whether the stock pays dividends or not?

What do you think: is it ever optimal to exercise an option early? Purchase of an American option rather than a European option confers the right to do this, but it comes at a higher premium cost. So there must be some point at which early exercise is optimal, or no one would buy American options. There can be only one possible benefit — the ability to receive cash flows earlier than the exercise date. However, if the option is being held as part of a hedging strategy, one gives up the "insurance" provided by the option when it is exercised early. Consider that you hold a large block of stock and a put to hedge against price declines. If the put is sold, you are then exposed to adverse price movements below the strike price of the put. The gain you realize by early exercise must at least offset the loss of the insurance.

16. What are the important factors affecting the value of an option?

The important factors include:

- **The "moneyness" of an option** — how close the underlying is to the strike price.

- **Time to expiration** — the longer the time to expiry, the higher the probability that the option will finish in the money.

- **Volatility** — this increases the value of the option for the same reason as above.

Other factors include risk-free rate and dividends paid (or foreign interest rate received if valuing currency option).

17. If the price of a stock increases by $1, how should the price of a call option change? What about a put option?

It depends on delta (noted by Δ, delta is the change in value of an option for a change in value of the underlying asset). If the stock is at or in the money, $\Delta = 1$ and there is a 1-for-1 relationship between c and S. But deep out of the money, it does not matter if the stock price goes up by $1, the call option will still be valueless. Only when we get sufficiently close to X so that $N(d_1) = \Delta > 0$ will changes in the underlying affect the value of the option. The same argument holds for a put, but the put has value only when S<X.

18. What is a warrant? Do warrants affect a firm's financial ratios such as ROE?

A warrant is a security similar to a call option on a stock, except a warrant usually has a much longer time to expiry. Warrants may often be attached to issues of preferred stock or bonds in order to make the issue more attractive to investors, as they offer the opportunity for some participation in stock appreciation. When the warrant is exercised, the owner pays the stated strike price in exchange for shares of stock. Thus, warrants result in the issue of new shares of common stock and are dilutive. All other things equal, measures such as ROE and EPS should decrease as the number of shares increases.

19. If Microsoft announces a new issue of 2,000,000 units at $120, with each unit consisting of one share of common, one share of preferred and a warrant for ¼ of a share of common, how many new shares of common will be issued assuming that the offering is successful and all warrants are exercised?

Each warrant entitles the owner to redeem it for ¼ shares, so since there were 2,000,000 warrants issued, there will be 2,000,000 (¼) = 500,000 new shares of common, in addition to the 2,000,000 new shares of common issued with the units, for a total of 2,500,000 new shares.

20. What would be a good instrument to use to hedge a portfolio of preferred stock?

Since preferred stock is similar to bonds that never mature (perpetual bonds), the best hedging instrument would be a long-maturity, risk-free instrument such as a T-bond option based on long-term treasuries.

21. If you are buying corporate bonds, which is more speculative: A, Aa, Baa or B?

B is the most speculative of these Moody's ratings.

22. If a client purchases a 6%, $1,000 bond selling at a yield to maturity of 7%, what is the amount of the semi-annual interest payment?

Yield is unimportant here. What's important is the coupon payment: 6% of $1,000. So each year the payout is $60, or $30 every six months (semiannually). Don't get confused if the interviewer adds extra information to the question.

23. Suppose you have an investment earning 1% per month. How do you convert this to an annual rate?

This question is simple, but on an interview, where you may be nervous, these simple questions can really trip you up. One should not assume that you won't be asked questions of this type just because they appear trivial. It is a good idea to talk through your thought process out loud and make use of a pad and paper if available. This "talk" might go something like the following:

Assuming that the client will earn a flat rate of r for each month over the year, then, if r is the monthly rate, this means that an investment of $P will be worth $P + interest on $P, or $P(1+r) after one month. This amount is invested at the beginning of the second month, so you will have ($P(1+r))*(1+r) at the end of the month. This process continues so that by the end of the year, you have a total of $P(1+r)^{12}$. The annualized interest earned is then $(1+r)^{12}$.

24. If you earn 6% a year using simple compounding, how would you calculate how much you would earn in a 90-day period?

You would just adjust this to account for the earning period. If you earn 6% using simple compounding, assuming (make sure to state your day count assumption here as day counts are very important on bond questions) 30/360 day-count convention, you would earn 6%*90/360 = 1.5% over a one-quarter period using simple compounding.

---

25. You have a client that wishes to be invested in a bond portfolio. Would you recommend short- or long-term bonds for this client, and why?

It depends on what you expect the yield curve to do. Is it upward sloping now and expected to flatten? Turn it around on the interviewer (though this can be dangerous as they can then turn it back on you) by asking, "What do you think interest rates are going to do?" But in general, remember that price of a bond moves inversely to yield. Thus if interest rates are expected to rise, the price of a bond should fall. Usually long-term bonds are much more sensitive to interest rate movements than are short-term bonds. So you would tend to stay on the long end of the curve in order to get the maximum profit from rate movements (also, of course, the maximum exposure/potential loss). So, if the client wanted to profit from a rise in interest rates, you might short the long bonds. If rates are expected to decline, you could buy the long bonds.

---

26. A client expects the market to move significantly and wants to hedge against either direction. What strategy would you recommend? Explain.

A straddle. This way, he will profit no matter which way the market moves. Note that if the market does not move, or moves but not by very much, the strategy will produce a loss. A straddle consists of the purchase of both a call and a put having the same strike price and expiry date. The upfront costs, apart from transaction costs, are the premiums that have to be paid for the call and put.

27. A client purchased a 10-year 5% par bond that will yield 6% if called at the first call date in 2 years. If the client holds the bond to maturity, what will the yield on the bond be? What if he sells the bond prior to maturity?

If he holds the bond to maturity, the client will receive a yield equal to the stated coupon rate of 5%. This is because he will receive par, he paid par and he is getting a 5% "return" in the form of coupon payments. He would only receive a yield other than this if the bond is surrendered prior to maturity. If the bond is called after two years, he would receive a yield of 6%; otherwise, the yield would have to be calculated based on the price of the bond when sold.

28. A corporate treasurer is borrowing at LIBOR to fund automobile loans. She wants to hedge against anticipated rises in the short rate. What hedging strategy would you recommend?

Enter an interest rate swap as the fixed rate payer/LIBOR receiver with swap dates arranged to coincide with borrowing dates.

29. What factors influence the price of a bond?

The main factors are the perceived risk of the bond, its yield and the issuer's cash flows.

30. If a fixed income client is interested in capital appreciation, in what type of interest rate environment should he buy bonds?

For capital appreciation you need the bond price to rise. Since bond prices are inversely proportional to yields, you need a falling interest rate environment.

> **31. A client in the 28% tax-bracket has a choice between a tax-free municipal bond yielding 7% and a corporate bond yielding 8.5%. Which should he choose? What would the yield on the corporate bond have to be in order to be equivalent to the tax-free bond?**

We have to compare the instruments on the same basis in order to decide. Since the muni bond is tax-free, the after-tax yield of the corporate bond is the comparator.

Let's take the corporate bond first and consider a one-year period for simplicity. Suppose the client invested $1,000 and earned 8.5%. Of this, 28% will be taxed so his gain is $(1-t)y\$1000 = (1-0.28)0.085*\$1,000 = 61.2$. This is equivalent to a tax-free yield of 6.12%. So, since the yield of the tax-free bond is greater than the after-tax yield of the corporate bond, he should choose the muni.

To determine the yield that will give parity between the corporate bond and the muni bond, use the formula "after tax yield on corporate = tax-free rate" or, $(1-t)y_{corp} = y_{tax-free}$, then $y_{corp} = y_{tax-free}/(1-t)$. For this example, the yield on the corporate bond would have to be $0.07/(1-0.28) = 9.722\%$ in order to be equivalent to the tax-free bond. If corporate bond yields are lower than 9.722%, choose the muni; otherwise, choose the corporate bond since the higher yield will offset the cost of the tax.

> **32. A convertible bond is selling at $1,200. It is convertible into 80 shares of stock. What would the stock price have to be for the convertible bond to be at parity with the stock?**

The value of the bond and the common stock must be equivalent at parity, so the stock must also be worth $1,200. Then the stock price would be $1,200/80 shares = $120/8 = 60/4 = $15/share.

33. The U.S. Treasury sells bonds at 1-year, 2-year, 5-year and 10-year maturities. You need the yield on a 7-year Treasury bond. How do you get it?

You would interpolate between known values. To get the value for the 7-year yield, you would interpolate between the 5- and 10-year yields. Linear interpolation would probably be sufficient, but splines and other smoothing techniques are sometimes used.

34. What are the factors affecting refinancing and prepayments of mortgages?

Not only the current level of interest rates, but also the path of rates: the level relative to prior levels and anticipated levels. General economic conditions: people tend to refinance in lowered interest rate environments. However, there is a "burn-out" effect whereby if people have refinanced, then rates rise and lower again, the pool of people refinancing may be diminished because those eligible to refinance have already done so earlier. Unpredictable events such as fires, divorces, marriages, relocations, winning the lottery and so on may also encourage people to sell homes and buy new ones.

35. How can you reduce the risk of a portfolio?

You add instruments for diversification. Hopefully these instruments are not well correlated with each other so overall they reduce risk. For equities, theoretically, you need about 30 different stocks for efficient diversification. There are many forms of risk: credit risk, liquidity risk, country risk, market risk, firm-specific risk and so on. You can also include hedging instruments. For example, if you own a particular equity, you could buy put options on it.

FINANCE GLOSSARY

Accretive merger: A merger in which the acquiring company's earnings per share increase.

Balance Sheet: One of the four basic financial statements, the Balance Sheet presents the financial position of a company at a given point in time, including Assets, Liabilities, and Equity.

Beta: A value that represents the relative volatility of a given investment with respect to the market.

Bond price: The price the bondholder (the lender) pays the bond issuer (the borrower) to hold the bond (i.e., to have a claim on the cash flows documented on the bond).

Bond spreads: The difference between the yield of a corporate bond and a U.S. Treasury security of similar time to maturity.

Buy-side: The clients of investment banks (mutual funds, pension funds) that buy the stocks, bonds and securities sold by the investment banks. (The investment banks that sell these products to investors are known as the "sell-side.")

Callable bond: A bond that can be bought back by the issuer so that it is not committed to paying large coupon payments in the future.

Call option: An option that gives the holder the right to purchase an asset for a specified price on or before a specified expiration date.

Capital Asset Pricing Model (CAPM): A model used to calculate the discount rate of a company's cash flows.

Commercial bank: A bank that lends, rather than raises money. For example, if a company wants $30 million to open a new production plant, it can approach a commercial bank like Bank of America or Citibank for a loan. (Increasingly, commercial banks are also providing investment banking services to clients.)

Commercial paper: Short-term corporate debt, typically maturing in nine months or less.

Commodities: Assets (usually agricultural products or metals) that are generally interchangeable with one another and therefore share a common price. For example, corn, wheat, and rubber generally trade at one price on commodity markets worldwide.

Common stock: Also called common equity, common stock represents an ownership interest in a company. (As opposed to preferred stock, see below.) The vast majority of stock traded in the markets today is common, as common stock enables investors to vote on company matters. An individual with 51 percent or more of shares owned controls a company's decisions and can appoint anyone he/she wishes to the board of directors or to the management team.

Comparable transactions (comps): A method of valuing a company for a merger or acquisition that involves studying similar transactions.

Convertible preferred stock: A relatively uncommon type of equity issued by a company, convertible preferred stock is often issued when it cannot successfully sell either straight common stock or straight debt. Preferred stock pays a dividend, similar to how a bond pays coupon payments, but ultimately converts to common stock after a period of time. It is essentially a mix of debt and equity, and most often used as a means for a risky company to obtain capital when neither debt nor equity works.

Capital market equilibrium: The principle that there should be equilibrium in the global interest rate markets.

Convertible bonds: Bonds that can be converted into a specified number of shares of stock.

Cost of Goods Sold: The direct costs of producing merchandise. Includes costs of labor, equipment, and materials to create the finished product, for example.

Coupon payments: The payments of interest that the bond issuer makes to the bondholder.

Credit ratings: The ratings given to bonds by credit agencies. These ratings indicate the risk of default.

Currency appreciation: When a currency's value is rising relative to other currencies.

Currency depreciation: When a currency's value is falling relative to other currencies.

Currency devaluation: When a currency weakens under fixed exchange rates.

Currency revaluation: When a currency strengthens under fixed exchange rates.

Default premium: The difference between the promised yields on a corporate bond and the yield on an otherwise identical government bond.

Default risk: The risk that the company issuing a bond may go bankrupt and "default" on its loans.

Derivatives: An asset whose value is derived from the price of another asset. Examples include call options, put options, futures, and interest-rate swaps.

Dilutive merger: A merger in which the acquiring company's earnings per share decrease.

Discount rate: A rate that measures the risk of an investment. It can be understood as the expected return from a project of a certain amount of risk.

Discounted Cash Flow analysis (DCF): A method of valuation that takes the net present value of the free cash flows of a company.

Dividend: A payment by a company to shareholders of its stock, usually as a way to distribute some or all of the profits to shareholders.

EBIAT: Earnings Before Interest After Taxes. Used to approximate earnings for the purposes of creating free cash flow for a discounted cash flow.

EBIT: Earnings Before Interest and Taxes.

EBITDA: Earnings Before Interest, Taxes, Depreciation and Amortization.

Enterprise Value: Levered value of the company, the Equity Value plus the market value of debt.

Equity: In short, stock. Equity means ownership in a company that is usually represented by stock.

The Fed: The Federal Reserve Board, which gently (or sometimes roughly) manages the country's economy by setting interest rates.

Fixed income: Bonds and other securities that earn a fixed rate of return. Bonds are typically issued by governments, corporations and municipalities.

Float: The number of shares available for trade in the market times the price. Generally speaking, the bigger the float, the greater the stock's liquidity.

Floating rate: An interest rate that is benchmarked to other rates (such as the rate paid on U.S. Treasuries), allowing the interest rate to change as market conditions change.

Forward contract: A contract that calls for future delivery of an asset at an agreed-upon price.

Forward exchange rate: The price of currencies at which they can be bought and sold for future delivery.

Forward rates (for bonds): The agreed-upon interest rates for a bond to be issued in the future.

Futures contract: A contract that calls for the delivery of an asset or its cash value at a specified delivery or maturity date for an agreed upon price. A future is a type of forward contract that is liquid, standardized, traded on an exchange, and whose prices are settled at the end of each trading day.

Glass-Steagall Act: Part of the legislation passed during the Depression (Glass-Steagall was passed in 1933) designed to help prevent future bank failure - the establishment of the F.D.I.C. was also part of this movement. The Glass-Steagall Act split America's investment banking (issuing and trading securities) operations from commercial banking (lending). For example, J.P. Morgan was forced to spin off its securities unit as Morgan Stanley. Since the late 1980s, the Federal Reserve has steadily weakened the act, allowing commercial banks such as NationsBank and Bank of America to buy investment banks like Montgomery Securities and Robertson Stephens.

Goodwill: An account that includes intangible assets a company may have, such as brand image.

Hedge: To balance a position in the market in order to reduce risk. Hedges work like insurance: a small position pays off large amounts with a slight move in the market.

High-yield bonds (a.k.a. junk bonds): Bonds with poor credit ratings that pay a relatively high rate of interest.

Holding Period Return: The income earned over a period as a percentage of the bond price at the start of the period.

Income Statement: One of the four basic financial statements, the Income Statement presents the results of operations of a business over a specified period of time, and is composed of Revenues, Expenses, and Net Income.

Initial public offering (IPO): The dream of every entrepreneur, the IPO is the first time a company issues stock to the public. "Going public" means more than raising money for the company: By agreeing to take on public shareholders, a company enters a whole world of required SEC filings and quarterly revenue and earnings reports, not to mention possible shareholder lawsuits.

Investment grade bonds: Bonds with high credit ratings that pay a relatively low rate of interest.

Leveraged buyout (LBO): The buyout of a company with borrowed money, often using that company's own assets as collateral. LBOs were the order of the day in the heady 1980s, when successful LBO firms such as Kohlberg Kravis Roberts made a practice of buying up companies, restructuring them, and reselling them or taking them public at a significant profit. LBOs are now somewhat out of fashion.

Liquidity: The amount of a particular stock or bond available for trading in the market. For commonly traded securities, such as big cap stocks and U.S. government bonds, they are said to be highly liquid instruments. Small cap stocks and smaller fixed income issues often are called illiquid (as they are not actively traded) and suffer a liquidity discount, i.e., they trade at lower valuations to similar, but more liquid, securities.

The Long Bond: The 30-year U.S. Treasury bond. Treasury bonds are used as the starting point for pricing many other bonds, because Treasury bonds are assumed to have zero credit risk take into account factors such as inflation. For example, a company will issue a bond that trades "40 over Treasuries." The 40 refers to 40 basis points (100 basis points = 1 percentage point).

Market cap(italization): The total value of a company in the stock market (total shares outstanding x price per share).

Money market securities: This term is generally used to represent the market for securities maturing within one year. These include short-term CDs, Repurchase Agreements, Commercial Paper (low-risk corporate issues), among others. These are low risk, short-term securities that have yields similar to Treasuries.

Mortgage-backed bonds: Bonds collateralized by a pool of mortgages. Interest and principal payments are based on the individual homeowners making their mortgage payments. The more diverse the pool of mortgages backing the bond, the less risky they are.

Multiples method: A method of valuing a company that involves taking a multiple of an indicator such as price-to-earnings, EBITDA, or revenues. Municipal bonds: Bonds issued by local and state governments, a.k.a., municipalities. Municipal bonds are structured as tax-free for the investor, which means investors in muni's earn interest payments without having to pay federal taxes. Sometimes investors are exempt from state and local taxes, too. Consequently, municipalities can pay lower interest rates on muni bonds than other bonds of similar risk.

Net present value (NPV): The present value of a series of cash flows generated by an investment, minus the initial investment. NPV is calculated because of the important concept that money today is worth more than the same money tomorrow.

Non-convertible preferred stock: Sometimes companies issue non-convertible preferred stock, which remains outstanding in perpetuity and trades like stocks. Utilities represent the best example of non-convertible preferred stock issuers.

Par value: The total amount a bond issuer will commit to pay back when the bond expires.

P/E ratio: The price to earnings ratio. This is the ratio of a company's stock price to its earnings-per-share. The higher the P/E ratio, the more "expensive" a stock is (and also the faster investors believe the company will grow). Stocks in fast-growing industries tend to have higher P/E ratios. Pooling accounting: A type of accounting used in a stock swap merger. Pooling accounting does not account for Goodwill, and is preferable to purchase accounting.

Prime rate: The average rate U.S. banks charge to companies for loans. Purchase accounting: A type of accounting used in a merger with a considerable amount of cash. Purchase accounting takes Goodwill into account, and is less preferable than pooling accounting.

Put option: An option that gives the holder the right to sell an asset for a specified price on or before a specified expiration date.

Securities and Exchange Commission (SEC): A federal agency that, like the Glass-Steagall Act, was established as a result of the stock market crash of 1929 and the ensuing depression. The SEC monitors disclosure of financial information to stockholders, and protects against fraud. Publicly traded securities must first be approved by the SEC prior to trading.

Securitize: To convert an asset into a security that can then be sold to investors. Nearly any income-generating asset can be turned into a security. For example, a 20-year mortgage on a home can be packaged with other mortgages just like it, and shares in this pool of mortgages can then be sold to investors.

Selling, General & Administrative Expense (SG&A): Costs not directly involved in the production of revenues. SG&A is subtracted from Gross Profit to get EBIT.

Spot exchange rate: The price of currencies for immediate delivery. Statement of Cash Flows: One of the four basic financial statements, the Statement of Cash Flows presents a detailed summary of all of the cash inflows and outflows during a specified period.

Statement of Retained Earnings: One of the four basic financial statements, the Statement of Retained Earnings is a reconciliation of the Retained Earnings account. Information such as dividends or announced income is provided in the statement. The Statement of Retained Earnings provides information about what a company's management is doing with the company's earnings.

Stock: Ownership in a company.

Stock swap: A form of M&A activity in whereby the stock of one company is exchanged for the stock of another.

Strong currency: A currency whose value is rising relative to other currencies.

Swap: A type of derivative, a swap is an exchange of future cash flows. Popular swaps include foreign exchange swaps and interest rate swaps.

10K: An annual report filed by a public company with the Securities and Exchange Commission (SEC). Includes financial information, company information, risk factors, etc.

Tender offers: A method by which a hostile acquirer renders an offer to the shareholders of a company in an attempt to gather a controlling interest in the company. Generally, the potential acquirer will offer to buy stock from shareholders at a much higher value than the market value.

Treasury securities: Securities issued by the U.S. government. These are divided into Treasury bills (maturity of up to 2 years), Treasury notes (from 2 years to 10 years maturity), and Treasury bonds (10 years to 30 years). As they are government guaranteed, often Treasuries are considered risk-free. In fact, while U.S. Treasuries have no default risk, they do have interest rate risk; if rates increase, then the price of UST's will decrease.

Underwrite: The function performed by investment banks when they help companies issue securities to investors. Technically, the investment bank buys the securities from the company and immediately resells the securities to investors for a slightly higher price, making money on the spread.

Weak currency: A currency whose value is falling relative to other currencies.

Yield to call: The yield of a bond calculated up to the period when the bond is called (paid off by the bond issuer).

Yield: The annual return on investment. A high-yield bond, for example, pays a high rate of interest.

Yield to maturity: The measure of the average rate of return that will be earned on a bond if it is bought now and held to maturity.

Zero coupon bonds: A bond that offers no coupon or interest payments to the bondholder.

Increase your T/NJ Ratio
(Time to New Job)

Use the Internet's most targeted job search tools for finance professionals.

Vault Finance Job Board

The most comprehensive and convenient job board for finance professionals. Target your search by area of finance, function, and experience level, and find the job openings that you want. No surfing required.

VaultMatch Resume Database

Vault takes match-making to the next level: post your resume and customize your search by area of finance, experience and more. We'll match job listings with your interests and criteria and e-mail them directly to your in-box.

> the insider career network™

About the Author

David Montoya: "David" (his pen name) is an associate with one the world's largest global investment banks. David received his MBA from the Stern School of Business at New York University, and received his Bachelors degree in Economics from the University of California at Berkeley. David has worked in Equity Research, Sales & Trading, and Corporate Communications.

Do you have an interview coming up with a financial institution?

Unsure how to handle a finance Interview?

Vault Live Finance Interview Prep

Vault brings you a new service to help you prepare for your finance interviews. Your 1-hour live session with a Vault finance expert will include an actual 30-minute finance interview, which will be immediately followed by a 30-minute critique and Q&A session with your expert.

Investment Banking/Corporate Finance Interview Prep

This session preps you for questions about:

- Mergers & acquisitions
- Valuation models
- Accounting concepts
- Personality fit for investment banking and corporate finance positions
- And more!

Sales & Trading Interview Prep

This session prepares you for questions about:

- Capital markets
- Macroeconomics, including impact of different pieces of economic data on securities prices
- Trading strategies
- Interest rates
- Securities including equities, fixed income, currencies, options, and other derivatives
- Personality fit for sales & trading positions
- And more!

challenging

What happens when great thinkers and doers from a variety of backgrounds come together? Typically, success is what happens. Winning in today's business world requires an intrinsic understanding of the unique needs and goals of very diverse customers in widespread markets. At American Express, the connection between the *diversity of our workforce* and our overall performance quality is clearly valued. We know it's *the link that enables us to drive competitive advantages* in the financial services industry.

For us, hiring *talented, dedicated go-getters* makes the measurable difference. We seek people who thrive on questioning traditional approaches and redefining accepted standards. Here, the status quo is always up for debate, and our team members are encouraged to share their *distinct perspectives and ideas* to help us reach our goal of becoming the world's most respected service brand.

A multi-billion dollar leader with diversified, global business operations, including travel, corporate and credit services as well as banking, insurance and accounting practices, *American Express is a happening place for ambitious people seeking exciting challenges!* To learn more about our dynamic company and our progressive initiatives in support of our diverse workforce, visit us at:

www.americanexpress.com/jobs

From left to right:

– *Sylvia Bass, VP, Rewards Business Development,
Consumer Card Services*

– *Bruce Shelton, Manager of Corporate Card Marketing
American Express Establishment Services*

– *Tareef Shawa, VP, Business Development, Global Travel*

– *Rachel Sha, Director
American Express U.S. Risk Management*

iversified financial services opportunities
around the corner
& around the world

American Express is an equal opportunity employer

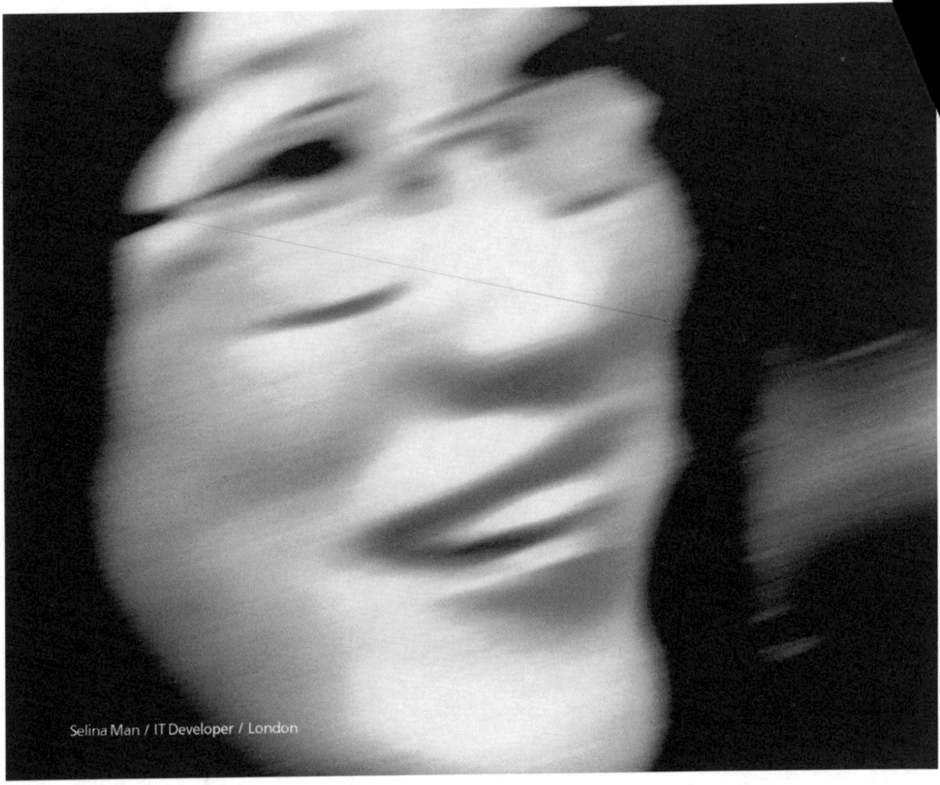
Selina Man / IT Developer / London

Unlimited global career opportunities

www.ubs.com

UBS Warburg

Global careers in investment banking

UBS Warburg is a business group of UBS AG. In the U.S., securities underwriting, trading and brokerage activities and M&A advisory activities are conducted by UBS Warburg LLC, an indirect subsidiary of UBS AG that is a registered broker-dealer and a member of the New York Stock Exchange and other principal exchanges and SIPC. In the U.K., these services are provided by UBS Warburg Ltd., a wholly owned subsidiary of UBS AG that is regulated in the U.K. by the SFA, to persons who are not private customers in the U.K.

One of our job requirements
includes "being yourself."

How can you grow as an individual if you're being forced into a mold?
At Ernst & Young, we empower you to push the boundaries. We offer
the chance to generate creative ideas that really count. On our teams
everyone has a role to play and something to contribute, so not only
do you have a voice but you can make a difference with clients and
co-workers alike. Break the mold.

FORTUNE
100 BEST
COMPANIES
TO WORK FOR 2002